COMBAT
HELICOPTERS

SINCE 1942

Steve Casey

BLANDFORD WAR PHOTO-FILES

COMBAT HELICOPTERS
SINCE 1942
KENNETH MUNSON & ALEC LUMSDEN

BLANDFORD PRESS
POOLE · NEW YORK · SYDNEY

First published in the UK 1986 by Blandford Press,
Link House, West Street, Poole, Dorset BH15 1LL

Copyright © 1986 Kenneth Munson and Alec Lumsden

Distributed in the United States by
Sterling Publishing Co., Inc.,
2 Park Avenue, New York, N.Y. 10016

Distributed in Australia by
Capricorn Link (Australia) Pty Ltd
PO Box 665, Lane Love, NSW 2066.

ISBN 0 7137 1756 4 (hardback)
ISBN 0 7137 1755 6 (paperback)

Typeset by Poole Typesetting (Wessex) Ltd.
Printed in Great Britain by Bath Press, Bath

British Library Cataloguing in Publication Data

Munson, Kenneth
   Combat helicopters since 1942. —(Blandford
war photo files)
   1. Military helicopters —History
I. Title II. Lumsden, Alec
623.77'6047   TL716

CONTENTS

INTRODUCTION

Why should the helicopter, once described as a 'clattering mechanical curiosity', now be regarded as an essential instrument of army or indeed naval activity? The helicopter is oddly like an extension of man himself: it is light and apparently frailly built, yet immensely strong for the purpose for which it is constructed but all too easily wounded. It can extend man's range of vision beyond the limited horizon allowed by his eye height of a little under six feet, to a distance limited only by the height to which the aircraft can climb.

Since the beginning of human history, man has needed to extend his horizon to guard himself from attack, quite apart from the need to search for food. When tribal fighting became an organised form of entertainment, there was a need for scouts to give warning of danger and to identify weak spots in the enemy's attack so that retaliation might be effective. As the range of available weapons was improved and extended beyond the convenient range of the eye, the hilltop observation posts which had been the natural solution to the problem had obvious limitations. It became necessary to observe the enemy and strike at him accurately and rapidly with missiles from a distance at least as far as the effective range of his own weapons, the story of David and Goliath being worth recalling in this context.

Finding better means to observe is a problem that has been tackled within recent history by a variety of means, including the use of captive observation balloons and man-lifting kites from the latter part of last century even up to the latter months of World War One. In the meantime, the aeroplane had become a practical proposition, taking over the longer range spotting tasks, observation balloons being essentially instruments for use in static or trench warfare.

The use, at first, of the telephone and, later, the wireless set, combined with aerial observation, enabled the old art of artillery spotting to be refined progressively so that, by the end of the 1914-18 war, the battlefield aerial vehicle had become an integral part of the artillery business.

Up to this stage, the spotter aeroplane had assumed for itself a role which was outwardly harmless. It was employed principally in communications and photography (although sometimes equipped with light bombs) but came to be regarded by the opposing forces as a serious menace. Following the 1918 Armistice in Europe, attention was turned to the use of aircraft for policing large tracts of sparsely inhabited territory by the colonial powers.

Apart from aerial police work, aircraft have played an increasingly important part in the conduct of military affairs, from local skirmishes between government forces and what used to be called 'dissident tribesmen', to the greatest war in history. The emergence in the 1940s of the close quarters aerial spotter or observation post, as opposed to the early concept of a relatively high altitude observer (for example, the armed two-seater types used by both sides in the Great War of 1914-18 and during the inter-war period by RAF Army Co-operation squadrons), gave some indication of the way things would have to go in the future, using cumbersome laid-out ground signals, message bags and pick-up hooks in the absence of adequate radio communications, whether secure or otherwise.

The diminutive, unarmed and utterly vulnerable lightplanes which were used on the Allied side during World War Two, such as the American Piper Cub and the British Auster, did remarkable work in spotting targets for artillery on all fronts. In doing so, they became targets themselves for both the enemy and their own missiles since, inevitably, they flew low and amid the shot and shell of both sides, quite apart from the small arms fire directed at them as fair game by the enemy and occasionally, in error, by their own side in the confusion of battle.

Observer pilots, for the most part artillery officers skilled in directing the targeting of batteries and correcting the fall of shells, displayed quite remarkable fortitude in sticking to a daunting task in the heat of battle. In doing so, they developed techniques which rivalled tracking and stalking while they hid from their enemy as they turned every piece of cover to their advantage. Thus, through their ability to fly slowly and turn rapidly, they were able almost to disappear from the enemy's view and suddenly to reappear very briefly and to give vital information to the Army's commanders, taking advantage of their underside camouflage.

Although the lightplane was the vehicle which made this activity possible and highly effective, it was not hard to predict its application to the helicopter. To use the ability to crouch out of sight behind cover close behind or beside the battle line until required is both prudent and economical in men and in materials.

The need to hide behind every piece of cover has become ever more important with the development of guided missiles, because the time safely at the spotter pilot's disposal for the vital action of obliterating a troublesome target is now exceedingly small. The phrase 'nap-of-the-earth flying' is very apt in the circumstances.

The skills developed by the artillery spotting fraternity have been put to even more dramatic use since the development of the guided weapon. The ability to hide until required to emerge into the open is now a critical faculty for the attack helicopter which has been brought to a high degree of effectiveness since early in the Vietnam war when the airborne anti-tank guided missiles became available. However, such missiles widely in use today are mostly wire-guided and relatively slow in their flight, demanding that the missile aimer retains a view of the target throughout the missile's flight. This can be as long as fifteen seconds, during which time the helicopter may be an uncomfortably sitting target and snap-shooting has therefore become of critical importance in, for instance, dealing with a massed tank attack.

The day of the 'fire and forget' missile, a 'smart' weapon which can home itself unerringly upon a selected target, has arrived, but such weapons, which are exceedingly expensive, are not yet available in significant numbers. It is, however, only a matter of time before they appear as a matter of course on the battlefield inventory.

The means of identifying targets in foul weather or darkness (or both, most likely), of selecting a particular target, and of aiming and delivering 'smart' missiles, is now readily available and increasingly to be seen as mast sights on the highest point on the helicopter – the top of the rotor head. Strange shapes giving Dalek-like images may now be seen cautiously peering above or between trees. The target seen by the enemy in such circumstances is little bigger than a football and, with the 'smart' missile in use, will be visible for very few seconds if the aimer is equally smart. Even the flight time of a wire-guided missile will require a very alert observer at the target to react exceedingly fast to do what little he can to counter the attack. A massed counter-attack by helicopter-borne

missiles against a massed attack by armour is likely to result in a considerable uproar, the battlefield becoming ever more dangerous, strewn with discarded control wires and the attendant risk of sprained ankles.

The 'crow's nest' has, since the earliest days of the sailing ship, been the place for spotting a landfall which, until radar, has been one of the most dangerous moments of a vessel's voyage. Equally, it has been the place for the sharpest eyes for spotting the approach of an enemy or a prize to be taken. As in any similar operation, the side which spots and identifies a target stands the best chance of winning an advantage. By the time farsighted planners of the military forces of technically advanced nations had recognised the unique potentialities of the rotary-winged aircraft, naval planners were thinking on similar lines.

The underwater menace of the mine, submarine and torpedo was clearly recognised from the time in the last century when the British Admiralty was persuaded that the whole concept of underwater warfare, initially regarded as unsporting, was acceptable. The reality of the submarine menace was brought home vigorously to governments and peoples when large numbers of merchant ships were sunk by mines and torpedoes in the Great War of 1914-18. Primitive countermeasures were initiated as soon as the threat was apparent, these ranging from masthead lookouts to coastal airships and seaplanes of essentially modest range, their patrol areas covering distances scarcely reaching more than 100 miles from shore.

The appalling losses of civilian lives that occurred at sea in World War Two caused a major expansion of the coastal and long-range maritime reconnaissance air services, particularly on the Allied side, in the search for German, Japanese and other hostile submarines. The problem to be faced was the need for long-range aircraft able to patrol the main convoy supply routes, in particular the North Atlantic. This inevitably meant adapting bombers for the job, which, in the 1940s, could ill be spared from the job they had been designed to do, or providing large numbers of fairly small escort aircraft carriers able to carry spotter aircraft armed with depth charges. The only way of spotting submarines was to look for the wake of a raised periscope or the surface trail of a speeding torpedo, easily seen on the surface by a ship in daylight and calm waters, but, by then, it was probably too late to do anything about it, particularly when the acoustic-homing torpedo became available. The good fortune to see a submarine on the surface, recharging its batteries while proceeding under diesel power, was rare. For the surface hunter, the antidote was Asdic, the under-water sounding device which in the hands of a skilful operator could give a fairly accurate bearing and distance of an underwater object, although the results could sometimes be frustratingly misleading.

At the present time, the helicopter is used by the authorities in most countries for a variety of purposes including Police, Coast Guard and land and sea search and rescue. The majority, however, are used by strictly naval and military forces and their aircraft have been developed on rather different lines from those used for civil and police operations. Because of the nature of the demanding uses to which the battlefield and naval helicopters are put, there is a similar accent on reliability in flight and the multi-engine helicopter tends to predominate.

As in any military situation, safety as such is not the principal criterion which determines the parameters of helicopter design. Nevertheless, the survivability of a helicopter and its occupants

'TAKE ME TO YOUR LEADER'. US Army Bell 406 OH-58D, AHIP, scout helicopters with mast-mounted weapon sights.

is obviously a very important matter. Experience gained in the Vietnam and Afghan wars, for example (and the latter can hardly be called anything else), has drawn attention to the need for armour protection of the crew and the need for the airframe to be able to function with quite severe battle damage. Even vital components such as rotor blades, the Achilles heel of the helicopter, and rotor gearboxes must be able to function with bits missing due to enemy action, even dry of lubricating oil. Much emphasis is now being placed upon the shielding and reduction as far as possible of infra-red sources to reduce the risk of strikes by IR homing missiles, or, alternatively, upon systems to decoy them harmlessly elsewhere. Considerable progress has been made in recent years in the use of glass, carbon and other fibres for the construction of primary structural members such as rotor heads and blades.

To get to the target of whatever kind and back, and to be able to find another target as quickly and efficiently as possible, is vital. Therefore, components must easily and quickly be replaced after damage. The flight time limitations of the older generations of rotor blades have been enormously extended by the new generation of materials whose fatigue life is many times greater than those previously used. The use of titanium has transformed the situation in highly stressed components in which steel was formerly used.

When considering the attack potentials of the combat helicopter, the requirements of land and sea forces are fundamentally different, even though they may broadly be achieved by the same basic vehicle. As previously mentioned, the army requirements are, initially, scouting to see where the enemy has got to, with the possibility of a quick strike against him – armed reconnaissance, in fact. The terms Combat Scout, Forward Edge of Battle Area (FEBA) for the defensively-armed helicopter and Forward Line of Own Troops (FLOT) for the attack aircraft have a particular significance. The situation having been established, the attack (which is the best form of defence) can then be worked out and attack helicopters armed appropriately.

The sighting systems for use in nap-of-the-earth operations have far outrun the Eyeball Mk 1, which now has the assistance of either the Head Up Display (HUD), such as has recently been adopted by the US Army for some 830 of its OH-58 helicopters, or the helmet-mounted sight. Each has its proponents for particular situations, broadly anti-helicopter on the one hand and

anti-tank on the other. In addition to the weapons themselves, 'smart' or otherwise, laser-guided missiles or unguided rockets, multi-barrelled turret-mounted cannon and grenade-launcher, the battlefield helicopter carries fully-armed troops in numbers proportionate to its size and occasionally far more, as was the case of the only RAF Chinook to reach the Falklands in the 1982 campaign. Battlefield logistical support, carrying guns, ammunition, etc., as well as men, can be of paramount importance when rapid response is required.

Maritime reconnaissance is of the utmost importance to naval units, whether operating singly or as escorts to merchant ships. The Falklands campaign highlighted the imperative need for ship-based airborne early warning of attack by low-flying aircraft at the earliest possible moment, particularly when out of range of land-based aircraft. Just as important, perhaps more so, is protection against surface and submarine attack.

Even medium-sized as well as heavy helicopters carry an enormous punch, and a short-range frigate-based aircraft can carry dunking sonar, sonobuoys and homing torpedoes for attacking submarines. The larger helicopters can do the same thing but at a range of 400 miles or so from the mother ship. All types of helicopter can be equipped for search and rescue duties, including carrier 'plane guard' operations. Not to be overlooked is the rather more shady duty of mid-course correction of so-called cruise missiles, a matter on which the Soviet Union has so far gained some experience using its ship-borne helicopters.

It would be almost impossible to over-estimate the importance of the helicopter as a military or naval vehicle, for observation or offensive purposes. No operation could these days be properly mounted without the assistance of helicopters. They are, however, not easy to fly, even with autostabilisation and exceedingly difficult without it, except in the best of weather conditions.

The reasons are complex why the helicopter, as a vehicle, is not easy to control with the accuracy one has grown accustomed to expect but, put as simply as possible, the machine is inherently unstable and, without assistance from some kind of autostabilisation, must be flown manually every second of the time, with visual reference to some external point such as the horizon. This can be both tiring for the pilot and difficult to co-ordinate at first.

A fixed-wing pilot, moderately experienced in

the natural stability of an aeroplane which goes roughly where it is pointing and stays approximately in the attitude in which he puts it (rightly or wrongly), may be handed over the controls of a light, simple helicopter while at the hover in still air and be told to keep it motionless, above a chosen spot and about six feet above the ground. Such an experience can be not only daunting but positively galling since the exercise appears at first to be quite impossible. The thing behaves like one possessed, probably begins to swing like a pendulum while the novice over-corrects in various ways, positively making matters worse with every swing until a kindly (or irate) instructor restores order and commands a further attempt, to the chagrin and immense relief of the by now thoroughly alarmed trainee.

Autostabilisation was one of the greater benefits bestowed upon the helicopter novice, wherewith to defy the Laws of Sir Isaac Newton and, incidentally, to make the greatest use of the remarkable properties of the helicopter, the ability to fly and hover in almost impossible weather conditions, particularly at night. The professionals, of course, make it appear easy and have undertaken prodigious feats of skill and heroism but, without autostabilisation, would have had far harder tasks to perform.

Automatic hovering is a feature of the present generation of helicopters which tends to be taken for granted. In a wide expanse of ocean, hovering while observing the results of a sonar dunk requires the relaxed attention of the crew to the results rather than an intense concentration on the means of achieving them. When it comes to the accurate placing of a 105 mm gun on an otherwise inaccessible spot or of placing a rescuer crewman on an exact spot, there is nothing to match human skill.

As for human courage, when it puts the helicopter to use as an extension of man himself, examples come readily to mind and include numerous rescues; these have been among the tree-tops in forest canopies, hauling up shot-down pilots and other casualties of war; with the rotor tips perilously close to a cliff face rescuing ill-advised climbers or beach-walkers; blowing away the smoke and flames from a stricken and burning ship which is about to blow up, so that survivors may escape; and, similarly on land, hovering above burning buildings so as to rescue people who would otherwise stand no chance of escape. Helicopters invite heroism and are well served by their crews in all services.

ABBREVIATIONS

AAM	Air-to-Air Missile
AH	Army Helicopter (British designation)
ASM	Air-to-Surface Missile
ASV	Air-to-Surface Vessel
ASW	Anti-Submarine Warfare
AV-MF	Soviet Naval Air Force (*Aviatsiya Voenno-Morskovo Flota*)
BAOR	British Army of the Rhine
cg	centre of gravity
DASH	Drone Anti-Submarine Helicopter
DOSAAF	Voluntary Society for Assistance to the (Soviet) Army, Air Force and Navy (*Dobrovolnoe Obshchestvo Sodeistviya Armii, Aviatsii i Flotu*)
EW	Electronic Warfare
FLIR	Forward-Looking Infra-Red
HAR	Helicopter Air Rescue (British designation)
HAS	Helicopter Anti-Submarine (British designation)
HC	Helicopter Cargo (British designation)
HOT	High-sunsonic, Optically-guided, Tube-launched (missile)
HU	Helicopter Utility (British designation)
LAMPS	Light Airborne Multi-Purpose System (US Navy programme)
MAD	Magnetic Anomaly Detector
MMS	Mast-Mounted Sight
OTH	Over The Horizon
SAR	Search and Rescue
TOW	Tube-launched, Optically-tracked, Wire-guided (missile)
Vertrep	Vertical replenishment (of ships at sea)
V-VS	Air Forces of the USSR (*Voenno-Vozdushniye Sily*)
WARPAC	Warsaw Pact

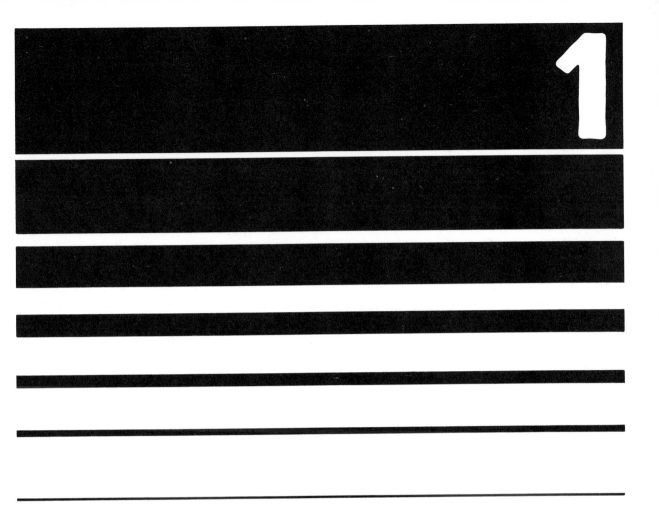

1

BLANDFORD WAR
PHOTO-FILES

GERMANY

Focke-Achgelis Fa 223 Drache (Dragon), 1939.
1. About 20 of these twin-rotor helicopters were built near Berlin in the middle years of World War Two. Most of them were destroyed in Allied air raids before they could be put to use in support of the German army. A handful survived and were eagerly examined by British, French, American and Russian designers. The progress made in Germany during the war was remarkable

considering the chaos caused to industry by bombing. The picture shows an Fa 223 hovering over wreckage, with a lifting frame suspended below the fuselage.

2. The twin-rotor arrangement of the Fa 223 resulted in a complicated drive system. The wire-braced undercarriage struts also provided bearings for the rotor drive shafts. The engine

was a 1,000 hp Bramo 323Q-3 air-cooled nine-cylinder radial.

Flettner Fl 282 Kolibri (Humming Bird), 1941.
3. Germany's Anton Flettner flew his first rotary-wing aircraft in 1932. Nine years later came the first of 24 Fl 282 prototypes, a two-seat helicopter with a 160 hp BMW-Bramo Sh 14A engine driving two 11.96 metre diameter

1

2

intermeshing rotors. Plans for BMW to build 1,000 were frustrated but the unarmed prototypes entered service in German warships in the Baltic, Mediterranean and Aegean from 1942. An improved Fl 285, able to carry two small bombs or depth charges, was under development when the war ended.

Focke-Achgelis Fa330 Bachstelze (Wagtail), 1942.

4. This little unpowered autogyro was built in some numbers in World War Two for use as elevated observation platforms, soaring some 400 ft above and behind towing U-boats, extending the horizon of the vessel's commander from a normal surface distance of about 12 miles to a little over double that distance. The advantage to the submarine of advance warning of the approach of a merchant convoy or attacking destroyer or frigate could be critical in the cat and mouse game on the open oceans. Unfortunately for the Fa330's pilot, a crash-dive could leave him abandoned, probably to drown.

3

4

Messerschmitt-Bölkow-Blohm BO 105 PAH-1, 1967.

5. The BO 105 is a remarkably agile light utility helicopter produced in liaison, observation and anti-tank (PAH, Panzerabwehr Hubschrauber) versions. The PAH can carry six Euromissile HOT missiles, a stabilised sight for which is mounted above the co-pilot's seat. The compact size and high degree of manoeuvrability make it a useful launching platform for HOT.

6. For groundfire suppression, the BO 105 can carry the 20 mm Oerlikon cannon. Ammunition is fed via external chutes from the fuselage (illustrated).

7. As an alternative to HOT missiles, the BO 105 can carry up to eight TOW missiles as seen here, showing the gunner's roof-mounted sight.

5

6

8. A maritime ASW version of the BO 105 is seen here, operated by the Colombian navy. Flotation air bags are mounted on the undercarriage skids ready for instant deployment in emergency.

9. Used by the West German anti-terrorist police, the very agile BO 105 needs a restraining hand in such delicate circumstances.

8

9

**Messerschmitt-Bölkow-Blohm / Kawasaki
BK 117, 1979.**
10. A joint collaborative programme which combines the previously separate projects, the MBB BO 107 and the Kawasaki KH-7, the BK 117 embodies a number of components of the BO 105, including rotor head and hydraulic boost system. The transmission is by Kawasaki. Costs are divided equally and prototypes flew in each country in 1979. The BK 117 is an 8-11 seat multi-purpose helicopter. The power plant is two 550 shp Avco Lycoming LTS 101-650B-1 turboshaft engines. The BK 117A-3M (illustrated) appeared in 1985 as a purely German multi-role military version of this successful design. It can be armed with a 12.7 mm / 0.50 in ventral gun turret, eight HOT anti-tank missiles, and a mast or roof sight.

FRANCE

2

Aérospatiale SA 313 Alouette II (Lark), 1955.
11. One of the earliest small helicopters, the Alouette II was also one of the most successful. Produced in several versions, the early Alouette IIs were powered by a 360 shp Turboméca Astazou II derated from 530 shp and useful in hot and high conditions, over 1,300 being ordered by 46 countries, including a later version powered by an 870 shp Artouste IIIB turboshaft derated to 550 shp and more suitable for hot conditions. They are used for carrying wire-guided AS 10 and AS 11 anti-tank missiles as well as for light transport and, as seen here, as an anti-tank trainer in a French army unit.

12. Close to the jaws of a gigantic and melting iceberg, this Alouette II is rather outside the hot and high environment to which it is best suited.

11

12

Aérospatiale SA 319B Alouette III (Lark), 1959.
13. A larger and more powerful development of the Alouette II utility helicopter, the Alouette III can carry six armed troops or two stretchers and two attendants.

14. Powered by an 870 shp Turboméca Astazou XIV turboshaft, the Alouette III has a reserve of power which can be useful in Search and Rescue (SAR) situations, as demonstrated here by a Netherlands naval unit.

13

14

15. In its maritime version, the Alouette III can carry two homing torpedoes and Magnetic Anomaly Detector (MAD) equipment for detecting and attacking submarines.

16. The Alouette III is able to carry a wide range of air-to-ground weapons, including (seen here) the AS 11 anti-tank weapon, or two AS-12 air-to-surface missiles.

Aérospatiale SA 321 Super Frelon (Hornet), 1962.
17. At the beginning of the 1960s, the French armed services required a heavy-lift helicopter, particularly to replace the large numbers of Piaseckis, and to be powered by turbines. The Sud Aviation Super Frelon resulted, powered by three 1,550 shp Turboméca Turmo III turboshafts. Like the Sikorsky Sea King in general appearance, the 23-foot long body and rotor transmission were the result of collaboration with the American company. The six-blade rotor was developed from Sikorsky's designs. A total of 99 was built. Used as a military transport, it can carry up to 30 troops or 11,000 lb of internally stowed or underslung freight. The rear ramp, which can be opened in flight, permits the loading of vehicles, weapons and personnel.

15

16

17

18. Besides the French naval air service, the Super Frelon has been exported to China for naval use. This example is seen on board the 'Dajiang' class submarine support ship J506.

19. As a naval helicopter, the Super Frelon can carry a wide range of search and attack equipment. This example, an SA 321G, is operated by Flottille 32 of the Aéronavale.

18

19

Aérospatiale-Westland SA 330 Puma, 1965.
20. The Puma is a twin-engined medium-sized tactical and logistics helicopter, first proposed by the French army in 1962. It was one of the three helicopters (with the Gazelle and Lynx) which were the subject of the Anglo-French helicopter agreement signed in 1968. It can carry up to 20 fully-armed troops and has a cargo floor suitable for heavy military loads.

21. The Puma can carry a two-ton externally slung military load, an example of which is the combination of the Swingfire long range anti-tank guided weapon and the Argocat lightweight cross-country wheeled vehicle seen in this picture.

20

21

22. The Puma's twin-wheeled undercarriage is retractable. The helicopter can be armed with side or axial-mounted machine guns or cannon. It can also fire AS 11, AS 12 or HOT anti-tank missiles.

23. The Puma's power plant comprises two Turbomeca Turmo IVC turboshaft engines. Air-cleaning filters and particle separators are installed on the Puma illustrated.

22

23

Aérospatiale-Westland SA 341 Gazelle, 1968.
24. One of three aircraft covered by the Anglo-French helicopter agreement of 1968, the Gazelle light utility aircraft seats five including crew. The *'fenestron'* tail rotor is largely responsible for it being rather quieter than most helicopters. The three-blade main rotor is of plastic-composite construction, designed in collaboration with MBB.

25. With a rotor system powered by an 858 shp Turboméca Astazou XIVH turboshaft, the Gazelle is widely used in the British and French armed forces as a light attack, utility and training aircraft carrying up to six HOT weapons, as seen here, cannons or rockets. Two much-modified Gazelles, with formidable if improbable armament, appeared in the Columbia film *Blue Thunder*.

Aérospatiale SA 315 Lama, 1969.
26, 27. In 1972, the Lama created a world height record for helicopters of 40,800 ft. Basically an Alouette II powered by a Turboméca Artouste IIIB turboshaft derated from 870 to 550 shp, and with power to spare, the Alouette III's strengthened rotor system, it carried four passengers and a pilot or, as a flying crane, could lift a ton. It was used in hot and high conditions.

24

26

27

Aérospatiale SA 365, 366 Dauphin 2, 1975.
28. The Dauphin and its twin-engined Dauphin 2 variant were designed as successors to the Alouette III. It is built for military, naval and Coast Guard duties. A development Mk 1 with gyro-stabilised sighting system is illustrated.

29. The Panther military version of the Dauphin 2 can mount a wide variety of weaponry and act as a high-speed assault transport for eight-ten commandos. It can carry, on the fuselage side mountings, packs of SNEB 68 mm rockets or eight HOT missiles, with a roof-mounted VENUS fire-control system for night-time anti-tank warfare. It has 912 shp Turboméca TM 333-1M turboshafts.

30. The naval SA 365N variant of the Dauphin 2 has completed deck-landing trials. Built to operate from small warships, it has folding rotor blades. It carries four AS 15TT anti-ship missiles and has a roll-stabilised Agrion 360 degree radar.

31. The SA 366 for the US Coast Guard, by whom it is known as the Dolphin, is equipped for SAR duties and the usual all-weather preventive operations and is powered by two 680 shp Avco Lycoming LTS 101-750A-1 turboshafts.

28

29

Aérospatiale AS 332 Super Puma, 1978.
32. The Super Puma is a derivative of the SA 330 Puma with more powerful engines and uprated transmission. The landing gear has been strengthened and the whole aircraft has an improved capability of surviving battle and crash damage. It can carry the usual tactical and anti-tank weapons, 21 troops or a slung load of 9,900 lb.

33. The Super Puma is an all-weather helicopter and the composite construction rotor blades are de-iced. The power plant is two 1,535 shp Turboméca Makila turboshaft engines. Greater power and lower fuel consumption than the earlier Puma enable it to have a long radius of action, better manoeuvrability in nap-of-the-earth operations and to perform less demanding missions on one engine only. A naval version of the Super Puma can carry two Exocet AM 39 anti-ship, all-weather sea-skimming missiles.

32

33

3

BLANDFORD WAR
PHOTO-FILES

ITALY

Agusta A106, 1965.
34. A small light helicopter designed for the anti-submarine role, the A106 unusually was a single seater, could carry two torpedoes and was intended to be carried on board frigates. It was an interesting idea which proved to be impractical and did not enter service with the Italian navy as had been proposed.

Agusta-Bell 212 Twin Two-Twelve, 1971.
35. The EW version of the twin-engined Agusta-Bell development of the Model 205, as used by the Italian navy, showing the large scanner mounted above the cabin roof. This shot shows the location of the inflatable flotation bags.on the landing gear skids.

34

35

Agusta-Bell 212ASW Twin Two-Twelve, 1971.
36. The Model 212 was derived from the 205, able to carry 14 troops, but, originally at the suggestion of the US Army, powered by two turboshaft engines giving a combined shp of 1,800. The engines are Pratt & Whitney Canada PT6T-3B as a Twin Pac. The 212 ASW version developed by Agusta is illustrated aboard the Italian destroyer *Audace*. It carries search radar, variable depth sonar and weapons for detecting and attacking surface ships as well as submarines.

Agusta A109, 1971.
37. A high performance twin-engined helicopter powered by two 420 shp Allison 250-C20B turboshaft engines for scout, light utility and light attack roles, it can carry up to seven troops (it has sliding doors for rapid troop disembarkation) and, in the attack mode, eight TOW or six HOT missiles, with a roof mounted sight, or pairs of light or heavy machine guns or rocket pods. Universal attachments for anti-tank missiles simplify mounting procedures that can be carried out in operational zones.

Agusta-Sikorsky Sea King SH-3, 1967.
38. Agusta has been building under licence the SH-3 in various versions from the SH-3D of 1967 up to today's SH-3H in the ASV/SAR role for the *Marinavia*. The Grupelicot 1 and 3 have been based aboard the new carrier *Giuseppe Garibaldi* from 1985 (illustrated). These can be armed with the OTO Melara Marte Mk 2 ASM system.

Agusta A129 Mangusta (Mongoose), 1983.
39. A close-up showing a turreted gun with belt-fed ammunition under the nose, four-missile TOW pods at each wing-tip and 19-tube launchers for 2.75-inch rockets under each wing.

37

40. Due in service in 1987, the A 129 is a dedicated battlefield helicopter like the *Hind* and Apache, but presents a smaller target. It is optimised initially for ground attack and anti-tank roles. A more lightly armed scout version is among other models being developed. The Mangusta has an integrated multiplex system which monitors and controls all of its mechanical, electrical, electronic and weapon systems, managing in flight all day and night missions via advanced infra-red technology, giving the helicopter round-the-clock readiness in darkness, bad weather and poor visibility.

The A129 can carry several weapons configurations, depending upon task. Alternatives can include eight HOT missiles or six Hellfires instead of the TOWs: two Stinger air-to-air missiles for air combat or self-defence; gun pods (7.62, 12.7 or 20 mm) instead of the rocket launchers; or rocket pods on all four pylons. In the nose housings are a pilot's night vision system and forward-looking infra-red (FLIR) sensor for night operations.

40

4

**BLANDFORD WAR
PHOTO-FILES**

GREAT BRITAIN

Avro (Cierva) C.30A, C.40 Rota I and II, 1933.

41. The Cierva C.30A autogiro was built by Avro and its first customer was the RAF which gave it the name Rota, having ordered ten (later twelve) to Spec. 16/35. They were delivered to the School of Army Co-operation from December 1934 onwards for training Army observers in artillery spotting from the air and other liaison duties. The prototype C.30 was modified to be able to 'jump-start' by connecting the engine to the rotor through the 'Autodynamic Head', over-speeding it briefly to allow a vertical take-off. This became the C.40 and the RAF ordered five as Rota Mk IIs, to Spec. 2/36; the first of them is seen here. During the war, the Rotas plus some impressed civilian C.30As were used round the UK coast for radar calibration as well as for Army spotter training.

Bristol 171 Sycamore, 1947.

42. The Sycamore, designed under the leadership of Raoul Hafner, starting in 1944 was, in its Mark 2 and subsequent forms, powered by an Alvis Leonides of 550 hp. It was a five-seater and was supplied to the British Army and to the RAF, as well as to the armed services of West Germany, Belgium and Australia. A capable and reliable helicopter, the Sycamore was notable

41

42

for being the first British rotary wing aircraft to be awarded a civil Certificate of Airworthiness. It performed well in support of the British Army and RAF during the troubles in Malaya in 1954 and in Cyprus, Kenya and Aden.

Westland-Sikorsky WS-51 Dragonfly, 1948.
43. Westland Aircraft built the S-51 under licence, powered by a 520 hp Alvis Leonides. It was used by the RN on planeguard duties with a port-side rescue winch.

44. RAF Dragonflies performed valuable casualty evacuation service in support of British troops in Malaya in the latter half of 1950, seen here about to lift a casualty from a jungle clearing.

43

44

45. Trials of the first Sikorsky S-51 operated by the Royal Navy were conducted aboard the 7,000 ton Royal Fleet Auxiliary ship *Fort Duquesne*, operating from a small platform mounted over the stern. The trials proved the practicability of the 300-mile range S-51 as a replacement for ship-based amphibians such as the Sea Otter.

Westland (Saunders-Roe) W.14 Skeeter, 1948.
46. Designed to meet a Staff requirement for the British Army, this diminutive two-seat helicopter was used in quite large quantities both in the United Kingdom and in the British Army of the Rhine, as shown here. It survived early resonance troubles but, with only a little under 200 hp at its disposal, did not have a sparkling performance. Nevertheless, it performed well in the light reconnaissance, training and communications roles. Though used principally by the British, a small number was supplied to the West German Bundeswehr and Navy. The engine was either a Gipsy Major 200 or a Blackburn Bombardier 702, each of about 180 hp.

FORT DUQUESNE
LONDON

Bristol (Westland) 173.192 Belvedere, 1952.
47. The Bristol 173 was, in effect, two Sycamores joined together with the same power plants and rotors linked so as to provide a measure of single-engine safety. The Alvis Leonides and Leonides Major engines tried at first were not suitable and coupled with persistent transmission and control troubles, the twin-tandem design was extensively modified, becoming the Type 192

powered by Napier Gazelle turbine engines. In its final form and named Belvedere by the RAF, it was ordered in small numbers as the world's first operational helicopter of this kind. It could carry up to 25 troops or up to 5,250 lb as a crane. Belvederes of No. 66 Sqn, RAF, made the longest unrefuelled over-water flight by helicopters from Singapore to Kuching in Sarawak and thence to Borneo in support of British troops.

During the campaign in Borneo in 1963, the RAF's Belvederes performed phenomenal feats of lifting in hazardous jungle environment, raising 105 mm guns, damaged Whirlwinds and other large and ungainly loads.

46

47

Westland WS-55 Whirlwind, 1952.
48. The Royal Navy received 25 S-55s in 1950. Following evaluation of these, Westland acquired a licence to build the aircraft. After the first ten, which had Pratt & Whitney engines, the Alvis Leonides Major, derated to 750 hp, was used. Shown here is one of the earliest of the S-55s acquired by the Royal Navy lifting the battered remains of another RN Whirlwind from a jungle clearing.

49. The Westland-Sikorsky Whirlwind HAS Mk 7 was used widely as a Commando transport and a flight is here seen aboard HMS *Bulwark* emplaning Royal Marine Commandos.

50. As well as planeguard duties, the Whirlwind was busily engaged in the jungle warfare in South East Asia in 1964. Here, an HAS Mark 7 takes off from a jungle clearing in the course of operations by No. 846 Sqn, Royal Navy, from HMS *Albion*.

48

49

50

51. A WS-55 HAS Mark 7 over the Borneo jungle where the slightest hesitation on the part of the Leonides engine might have caused the No. 846 Sqn crew some concern.

52. A Royal Canadian Navy S-55 showing its dipping sonar and a homing torpedo. At close range this early Anti-submarine helicopter was a self-contained hunter-killer. A Sikorsky-built S-55 is illustrated.

53. A Royal Navy Whirlwind is carried onto the hangar deck by the deck lift, with its rotor blades folded.

51

Westland P.531-2 Scout, 1960.
54. The earlier of the 'twins' produced by Westland is the Scout. It is derived from a private venture by Saunders-Roe as a Skeeter replacement and, when Westland took over in 1959, the P.531 was developed first for the British Army. It was powered by a Blackburn A129, later to become familiar as the Bristol Nimbus turboshaft (later still, Rolls-Royce), producing 710 shp in its derated form. A British Army order for the Scout AH Mk 1 five-seater was made in 1960 and about 150 were delivered. They are fitted with a skid landing gear and powered by a Nimbus 101 or 102, derated to 685 shp. The intake is protected against the ingestion of sand and other damaging particles in arid areas. The Scout is used for light transport, as shown here carrying a slung load of oil drums, casualty evacuation, search and rescue and training. In addition when used in operations or training it can carry wire-guided anti-tank missiles.

Westland P.531 Wasp, 1962.
55. The Wasp was developed in parallel with the Scout but to a rather later time scale. It is a naval version of the original Saunders-Roe P.531, taken over by Westland in 1959, differing in having a

54

55

56

fully-castoring, quadricycle landing gear, a half tailplane on the top of the tail rotor pylon on the starboard side and a main rotor and tail boom that can be folded for stowage on board small ships. In addition to some 80 Wasp HAS Mk 1s used by the Royal Navy, others have been delivered to Brazil, Holland, New Zealand and South Africa. Their uses include anti-submarine patrol and training from ships and shore establishments.

56. The weapons which can be carried by the Wasp include two Mk 43 or 44 torpedoes slung between the undercarriage legs or two Mk 11 depth charges. Alternatively, two AS 11 or two AS 12 missiles may be carried.

57. The Wasp has been a familiar sight operating from the stern of Royal Navy frigates, an often inhospitable and dangerous environment. The fully-castoring, well-sprung four-point undercarriage copes with operating from a pitching, rolling, heaving deck. A Royal Navy Flight Deck Officer guides in HMS *Scylla*'s Wasp. The crewman facing backwards is *not* the pilot.

Westland WS-58 Wessex, 1957.

58. Westland acquired a licence to build the Sikorsky S-58 in 1956, importing an HSS-1 example powered by a Wright R-1820 radial engine, replaced by a 1,100 shp Napier Gazelle turboshaft. The WS-58 went into production, powered by a 1,450 shp Gazelle Mk 161. It began naval service trials in April 1960 as the Wessex HAS Mk 1 anti-submarine helicopter

equipped with a dipping sonar. It could be stripped to carry sixteen Marines or a 4,000 lb slung load in the assault role. The anti-submarine version carried two homing torpedoes or SS 11 wire-guided missiles, machine guns or 2-inch unguided rockets. The HAS Mark 3 was similar with a 1,600 hp flat-rated Gnome Mk 165, large radar dome and four crew for ASW search and strike duties (illustrated).

59. The Wessex HU Mk 5, similar to the high-performance Mark 2, was a Commando assault version like the Mark 1 for the RN and replaced piston-engined Whirlwinds. Single-engined variants were delivered to the Royal Australian Navy and twin-engined Wessexes to Iraq, Ghana and Brunei and The Queen's Flight of the RAF.

58

59

60

60. The Wessex HC Mk 2 had two coupled Rolls-Royce/Bristol Gnome turboshafts giving 1,550 shp at the rotor head. A substantial number was delivered to RAF Transport Command from 1964.

Westland WS-55 Series 3 Whirlwind, 1968.
61. The Series 3 Whirlwind is the Westland-developed WS-55 powered by a turbine engine, at first a Blackburn Twin Turmo, followed by a General Electric T58 turboshaft, licence-built as the Bristol Siddeley Gnome, which gave the Series 3 a slightly longer, more elegant nose. The Series 3, ordered for the RAF in 1968, became the HAR Mark 10. Many of the RN's piston-engined Whirlwind Mk 7s were re-engined with Gnomes, becoming HAR Mark 9s. The power of the Gnome enabled the Whirlwind to carry a one-ton underslung load. It could mount two machine guns or four AS 11 or Vigilant anti-tank weapons.

62. During operations against insurgent forces in North Borneo, the high power of the Gnome was particularly useful in adverse conditions when the Whirlwind was called upon to carry its full load of ten armed troops.

61

62

63. Many notable rescues have been made by RAF Whirlwinds, one of which is seen here in the course of a practice with an RNLI lifeboat.

Westland Sea King, 1969.
64. Westland acquired a licence agreement to build the Sikorsky S-61 in 1959, permitting Westland to use the airframe, transmission and rotors of the SH-3D. To replace the Wessex as a long-range anti-submarine helicopter in the Royal Navy, no major changes were made to the design of the aircraft. The fuselage remains basically similar to the S-61, retaining its amphibious capability. The first Sea Kings were HAS Mark 1 anti-submarine aircraft, completed in 1972 and powered by Rolls-Royce Gnome H.1400 turboshafts of 1,500 shp. The HAS Mark 2, seen here, was an uprated version with 1,660 shp Gnomes for ASW and SAR duties. The Sea King HAS Mk 5s of the RN (including updated Mark 2s) carry advanced radar and dunking sonar, the radar being carried in a larger dorsal radome than on earlier models and distinguished by a flat top.

63

64

65. A version of the HAS Mk 2, the HAR Mark 3 is in use by the RAF for search and rescue duties, using a winch and carrying a crew of four. It is capable of carrying nineteen people, or eleven and two stretchers, or six stretchers. Extensive navigation equipment, similar to that of the Royal Navy's Sea Kings, is carried in this aircraft.

66. The Falklands campaign of 1982 showed up the need for an airborne early warning system to guard against low-level attack. Under Project LAST (Low Altitude Surveillance Task), two Sea King HAS Mk 2s were modified to mount a Searchwater maritime surveillance radar on a retractable and inflatable cupola, similar in shape to a kettle drum, as seen here. Others were converted subsequently and are embarked in one of the Royal Navy's aircraft carriers for operations beyond the range of shore-based ASW aircraft. Further improvements are under way, involving the fitting of composite rotor blades and improved transmission, and mounting two Sea Eagle long-range ASMs.

65

66

Westland-Aerospatiale WG13 Lynx, 1971.
67. Introduced into service in 1976, the Lynx has been continuously uprated both in its army and naval versions. The latest Lynx Mk 7 has been ordered by the British Ministry of Defence for the Army Air Corps which has already taken 117 of 329 Lynx ordered world-wide; the naval equivalent, technically, is the HAS Mk. 3. Differing from earlier versions, the Mark 7 has improved transmission and 1,120 shp Rolls-Royce Gem 40 engines. The tail rotor is of composite construction, and rotates in the reverse direction (clockwise) to previous variants. This improves control and reduces the noise of the Lynx, a matter of significance in the battlefield for which the helicopter was designed to fulfil important anti-tank duties. The Mark 7 weighs 10,750 lb, an increase of 1,150 lb over earlier marks. The Army Lynx formation illustrated is launching a salvo of HOT anti-tank missiles.

68. New technology all-composite blades will become available for the Lynx. The Navy Lynx has, as its primary roles, attack on submarines and surface vessels as well as SAR. In the anti-surface vessel role, the Lynx can carry four Sea Skua homing missiles (illustrated) and electronic

67

68

warfare systems. As a submarine hunter, it can locate and classify underwater targets using dunking sonar. Its weapons can include depth charges and the new Sting Ray torpedo. Lynx was one of the three types of aircraft involved in the 1968 Anglo-French helicopter agreement, the others being Puma and Gazelle. Westland has design leadership in the Lynx programme.

69. Over 300 Lynx have been ordered for the British Army Air Corps (114 AH Mk 1 and nine AH Mark 5) and the Royal Navy (60 HAS Mark 2 and twenty HAS Mark 3), and by France (Navy, Mark 2 and fourteen Mark 4), Germany (Navy), Holland (Navy), Brazil (Navy), Argentina (Navy), Qatar (Police), Denmark (Navy), Norway (Air Force) and Nigeria (Navy). Sixty of the British Army's Lynx are equipped with eight TOW for an anti-tank role with BAOR. The AH Mark 1 and HAS Mark 2 and early export aircraft have Gem 2 engines, whereas later models have Gem 41 or 43 engines. A Royal Netherlands Navy Lynx is illustrated.

70. Lynx 3 is a private venture in the anti-tank role (HOT, TOW or Hellfire), with uprated Gem 60 engines, higher all-up weight and avionics for day/night/all weather operation, better survivability and Stinger AAMs for self-defence. As illustrated, an MMS (Mast-Mounted Sight) as well as an exhaust infra-red suppressor can be fitted.

Westland Commando, 1973.

71. A tactical helicopter based on the Sea King with similar payload and range performance, it has accommodation for up to 28 fully equipped troops or a slung load of up to 7,500 lb. Although the first production version was outwardly similar to the Sea King, the Mk 2 Commando has neither outboard sponsons nor radome and has been exported to Middle Eastern countries.

72. The Royal Navy utility version of the Commando Mk 2 is the Sea King HC Mk 4, retaining the six-blade tail rotor, the folding main rotor blades and rear fuselage of the Sea King HAS Mk 5 but the landing gear does not retract. The engines are Rolls-Royce Gnome 1400-1 turboshafts, totalling 2,700shp. The HC Mark 4 illustrated was engaged in the evacuation of Beirut in 1984.

70

71

Westland WG 30, TT 300, 1979.
73. The first military order was received late in 1985 for Westland's twin-Gem WG 30. Typically it carries fourteen fully equipped troops, a mortar, or Milan anti-tank missile team, or six stretchers with ten seated casualties or medical attendants, over a 100-kilometre (62-mile) stage length.

Vinten-Wallis Vindicator, 1984.
74. This is the latest development in the long history of autogyro development, a pilotless version of the Wallis WA-116. An RPV for Vinten cameras or other sensors, the Vindicator is powered by an 80 hp engine and can carry a payload of 353 lb.

73

74

5

UNITED STATES OF AMERICA

Kellett KD-1A, (0-60), 1934.
75. The Kellett Autogyro Corporation held a manufacturing licence from Cierva in Britain and made their first Autogiro, the KD-1, in 1931. After successful trials, the US Army Air Corps bought a KD-1A and subsequently acquired a further seven modified models, designated YG-1A and B, and seven YO-60s. The latter were powered by the 300 hp Jacobs R-915-3 radial.

Sikorsky VS-316A Hoverfly (UK), R-4, HNS, 1942.
76. Ordered in 1940 and first flown on 13 January 1942, the first practical helicopter operated by the US Army Air Forces and Navy, as well as by the RAF, was developed directly from the VS-300, Sikorsky's most successful experimental design. The R-4B two-seater had little reserve power for the kind of operation seen here — a hazardous landing on a ship's stern. As well as use by the US Army and Navy, some 45 were ordered by the British Air Ministry, serving in No. 529 Sqn, RAF, and No. 705 Sqn, Royal Navy, from August 1944. The pilot's seat was on the left side and the picture indicates the pilot's concentration.

77. A USAAF R-4B was used in one operation in World War Two when one was flown behind the Japanese lines in Burma to rescue four wounded British soldiers and a shot down pilot. The mission involved crossing a 5,000 ft mountain range and lifting one man at a time. The photograph shows the R-4B with the 10th Air Force in Burma on 23 January 1945.

76

77

Sikorsky VS-316B Hoverfly Mk II (RAF), R-6, HOS, 1943.

78. A developed and cleaned up version of the R-4, the R-6 was originally destined for the USAAF but was put into production largely on the instigation of the US Navy. It used the moving parts of the R-4 but a slightly more powerful Franklin engine of 245 hp. Quite the best-looking helicopter produced to date, it was used by all of the US armed services in small numbers and was given to the Royal Navy and RAF under the Lend-Lease Scheme. For collaboration with the British Army, some seventeen were delivered to the RAF and known as Hoverfly Mk II.

Sikorsky VS-327, R-5, H-5, HO3S, 1943.

79. A dramatic picture of a USAAF R-5A (43-46630) of the Air Rescue Service. The R-5 (later H-5) in Air Force and US Navy service first appeared with a tail wheel, as seen here. It was a two-seater powered by a 450 hp Pratt & Whitney R-985-AN-5 engine. Both versions were used with good effect in Korea, primarily on casevac duties. The VS-327 was the prototype of the later and successful S-51 or R-5F, a four-seater which had been reached via the three-seat R-5D. Westland built the S-51 as the Dragonfly.

78

79

Bell 47 Sioux, OH-13, HTL, HUL, 1945.

80. A simulated 'rescue' of an unserviceable Sioux by a Royal Navy Wessex typifies the ease of transport in emergency of the ubiquitous little three-seater.

81. Only very recently has the hum of the little Sioux become a rarity in European skies as piston powered helicopters have given way to turbine variants. Turbine power, ideally suited to the needs of the helicopter, began to take over in the late 1960s, as soon as technology enabled the fuel consumption for such small units to be economically acceptable. In its many forms, the Bell 47 was the subject of one of the longest ever production runs. It was extensively used by the US services for communication and casevac purposes, and was made immortal in the long-running M*A*S*H television series. The counter-balanced see-saw rotor system typified the early generation of Bell helicopters. Agusta in Italy built over 1,100 examples and it was built by Westland for the British Army (by which it was sometimes called the 'Iron Budgie') by whom it was mainly used as a training helicopter, as here.

Hiller UH-12 Raven OH-23, HTE, 1948.

82. A small two-seat observation helicopter comparable with the contemporary Bell 47 and characterised by an angled tail rotor drive shaft. Not to be confused with the US Army designation, UH stood for 'United Helicopters' and was a design of Stanley Hiller. The UH-12 was powered by a 200 hp Franklin piston engine when first built in 1948. From then onwards, over

2,200 of various models were built for training, light communications and casevac purposes as well as observation, notably in the Korean war from 1950. As a basic helicopter trainer, the UH-12 was widely used, in particular by the British Army and Royal Navy until replaced by the Westland-built Bell 47G4 Sioux. It went back into production in the late 1970s in four versions, two of them with turbine engines.

Piasecki (Vertol) PV-17, HRP-1, 1947.

83. The 'Flying Banana' was the first twin tandem rotor built by Piasecki (who became Vertol in 1956) and has evolved over the years into the Boeing Vertol Chinook familiar today. The HRP-1 with a fabric-covered fuselage was developed into the metal-skinned HRP-2. The rotor arrangement allowed easy cg loading limits. It was used in small numbers by the US Navy and

82

83

Marines. It was powered by a 600 hp Pratt & Whitney R-1340 radial. It could carry ten troops.

Piasecki (Vertol) PV-18 Retriever, Army Mule, HUP-1, 2, 3, H-25, 1949.
84. Designed as a utility helicopter to be based on board US warships, the HUP-1 was distinguished by the endplate fins on the rear stabilisers. It could carry four to five passengers in addition to the two-man crew. Power was by a 525hp Continental R-975 radial. The later HUP-2 had a rescue winch and anti-submarine radar but no rear fins. It was powered by a slightly more powerful engine of the same make. The Army Mule version was built for the Navy as the HUP-3. Some 300 of all versions were built. They performed valuable service in Korea in 1953.

Sikorsky S-55 Chickasaw, Whirlwind (see Westland) H-19, HO4S, HRS, 1949.

85. A major breakthrough in operating terms, the S-55 was the second Sikorsky helicopter to be built on a large scale and remained in production for a decade. Almost 2,000 were built by Sikorsky and licenced builders in Britain (Westland), Japan (Mitsubishi) and France (SNCASE). The early versions were powered by 600 hp Pratt & Whitney R-1340 engines but later these were replaced by 700 hp Wright R-1300 engines, a change which was recognisable by a slight downward sweep at the tail boom. The Chickasaw was extensively used by the US Army and Marine Corps for moving troops, on one occasion lifting a company of 228 Marines plus nine tons of supplies to the top of a 3,000 ft mountain during the Korean war. In another operation during the Korean War hard-working Chickasaws carried a battalion of US Marines into action in the front line in full view of opposing forces.

86. The H-19 was also used by the US Air Force; the H-19 seen here belonged to the Military Air Transport Service.

86

87. The Sikorsky S-55 was widely exported. The Israel Air Force operated several, the one here demonstrating the trawl net method of rescuing people from the sea, first designed by Cmdr J. Sproule, RN.

Kaman K-600 HOK. HUK, 1951.
88. An intermeshing twin-rotor helicopter derived from the HTK-1, the Kaman K-600 was used by the US Navy as the HUK-1 and by the Marines as the HOK-1. The power unit was a 600 hp Pratt & Whitney R-1340 radial. The crew was two and five passengers or two stretchers and two attendants.

Kaman K-240 HTK, 1951.
89. A small twin-rotor helicopter whose blades intermeshed in the way devised by German designer Anton Flettner. It was a three-seater used in small numbers by the US Navy as a trainer. The power unit was a 240 hp Lycoming 0-435.

87

88

89

Piasecki (Vertol) PD-22 (Vertol 42, 43, 44) Work Horse, Shawnee, Rescuer H-21, HRP2, 1952.
90. The fabric-covered, banana-shaped Piasecki HRP-1 (see photograph **83**) was developed into the metal-skinned HRP-2 Rescuer for the US Navy and then the H-21 in various versions for the USAF and US Army. An H-21 of the US Army is illustrated.

91. Known by a bewildering number of titles, the Work Horse was built in large numbers for export as well as for the US forces. A Model 44 operated by the Swedish Navy is illustrated.

90

91

92. The large and successful Piasecki (Vertol) transport was powered by a 1,425 hp Wright R-1820 radial. Illustrated is a CH-21C Shawnee used as rescuer by the Canadian Armed Forces for lifting a slightly bent Cessna 180 from the frozen surface of a lake.

Bell 61, HSL-1, 1953.
93. Bell's tandem-rotor HSL-1 was designed for anti-submarine warfare, carrying sonar, two Petrel air / underwater missiles or 800 lb of depth charges. Too noisy for ASW work, it entered US Navy service for second-line duties after the Korean war. The engine was a rear-mounted 1,900 hp Pratt & Whitney R-2800 radial.

Sikorsky S-56 Mojave, HR2S, H-37, 1953.
94, 95. The first serious American attempt to develop a single-rotor 'flying crane' was the big S-56, powered by two Pratt & Whitney R-2800 radials, an assault helicopter intended for the US Marine Corps, although more were built for the Army. An electric winch of nearly one ton capacity assisted in loading clam-shell nose doors; 24 troops could be carried.

Sikorsky S-58 Choctaw, Seabat, Seahorse (Wessex) H-34, HSS, HUS, 1954.
96. In 1952, the US Navy required a replacement for the S-55 as an anti-submarine helicopter. The first of 258 HSS-1s was delivered in 1955, since when 1,821 were built until production ceased. The HSS was later redesignated SH-34. The only difference between the CH-34A and C was in the equipment fitted. The S-58 could carry up to

sixteen troops or, used as a crane, nearly 3,000 lb as a slung load. The power unit of the S-58 was a 1,525 hp Wright R-1820 but, although the Westland Wessex version had been turbine-powered for several years, a turbine-powered version for the civil market using the Pratt & Whitney PT6T Twin Pac did not become available until 1970. Among several versions produced for the US Navy, the SH-34G was named

94

95

Seabat. This carried dunking sonar search equipment and anti-submarine weapons. Auto-stabilisation equipment was fitted to the J version for night operations. The US Marines used the S-58 as the UH-34D and E, calling it the Seahorse. Many are seen here on board USS *Antietam*. About 500 S-58s were used by the US Marines. Uses included lifting US satellites from the sea. The US Army used large numbers under the name Choctaw. In addition to the aircraft built under licence by Westland as the Wessex, the S-58 was built under licence in France by Sud Aviation (166) and twenty were assembled in Japan by Mitsubishi.

Bell, Agusta-Bell 204, 205 Iroquois, 'Huey' HU-1, UH-1, 1956.

97. The justly famous 'Huey' acquired its name from its original US Army designation HU-1. This name for the Bell 204, rather than Iroquois, stuck with the troops. The designation HU-1 was amended to UH-1 in 1962, some three years after the US Army began to receive the utility, casualty evacuation and training helicopter.

98. The Vietnam war was the opportunity for the Huey to show its paces. In its early form, the HU-1B, with a 1,100 shp Lycoming T53 turboshaft engine, could carry seven troops.

97

98

99. From the start of its career with the US Army, the Huey has been used as a utility helicopter and can easily lift a 2,600 lb Jeep and its crew up to the front line.

100. An inviting target but not likely to be repeated in a war situation if it could be avoided, a flight of Hueys on an exercise in South Korea.

99

100

101. Casualty evacuation has been an essential function of the UH-1, particularly in the various wars from Vietnam onwards. Here, a Vietnamese soldier desperately clings to the landing skid of a Huey hovering just clear of undergrowth on a steep hillside.

102. Succeeding the UH-1B came the UH-1D, the military equivalent of the Bell 205. It had a larger cabin seating twelve to fourteen troops. Here, a combat team leaps from a hovering Huey into Vietnamese undergrowth. Over 7,000 Bell UH-1s of many varieties have been built and, with a blade improvement programme using composites, the US Army expects at least 2,700 of those up to the current UH-1H standard to remain in service beyond the year 2000. Hueys have been built in large numbers both in Italy by Agusta and (1,400 shp Lycoming T53-L-13) in Japan by Fuji.

101

102

103. A US Army UH-1B armed Huey launches a French Nord AS 11 guided missile. The helicopter could also mount four 7,62 mm M-60 machine guns for discouraging enemy groundfire, and four anti-tank missiles of various kinds.

Hiller Rotorcycle YROE-1, 1958.
104. One of the lightest helicopters ever built, the Hiller YROE-1 Rotorcycle weighed 300 lb empty and could be dismantled and carried into battle in a portable container. Designed in 1958, it was evaluated by the US Marine Corps but not adopted for service.

Boeing Vertol 107, CH-46 Sea Knight, 1958.
105. Conceived as a medium transport helicopter, the Model 107 was the first design to emerge following the change of the Piasecki Helicopter Corporation in 1956. A total of 624 of the type was built during 1964-71. It features a rear loading ramp and power-operated rotor folding system. It can carry up to 25 armed troops.

106. As a medium-lift helicopter in Vietnam, the Sea Knight operating with the US Marines performed with distinction. An example is seen lifting a damaged UH-34 Seahorse from a jungle clearing. It can carry a 4,000 lb slung load.

107. The CH-46 is seen here undertaking Vertrep duties at sea from the US Fleet support ship *Sacramento* to a carrier with an underslung load of torpedoes.

108. In July 1985, Boeing Vertol started delivery of 354 new Safety, Reliability and Maintainability improvement kits to extend the life of Sea Knights well into the 1990s. The Sea Knight is still being built in Japan by Kawasaki as the KV107, and is used by the Japanese Navy as a specialised minesweeper. A version is used on SAR duties by the Canadian Armed Forces, as seen here. The two engines are 1,250 shp General Electric T58-GE-8 turboshafts.

Kaman K-600-3, H-43, Huskie, 1958.
109. The Huskie intermeshing twin-rotor helicopter was the last of the line of aircraft built by Kaman after the designs of Anton Flettner. It was the winner of the USAF competition for a local crash rescue helicopter, both for the rescue of survivors (up to eleven) and for fire suppression. Developed from the HOK/HUK series, the H-43 was at first powered by a Pratt & Whitney R-1340. To improve the load-carrying capabilities of the Huskie, the Lycoming T53 shaft turbine was fitted, giving it 860 shp. This model was designated H-43B and became a familiar sight around the airfields where the USAF operated, particularly in Britain and in Europe, earning itself inevitable names like the 'egg-whisk'. In all, 416 Kaman twin-rotor helicopters were built, including HOK, HUK and HTK.

110. A Kaman H-43B of the US Air Force Rescue Service.

109

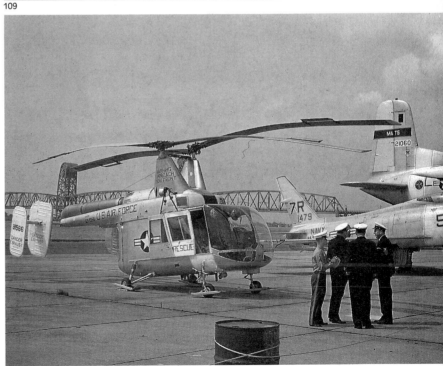

110

Kaman K-20, SH-2, HH-2 Seasprite, 1959.
111. The Seasprite won a US Navy competition in 1956 for a fast, long-range utility and SAR helicopter capable of operating in all weather conditions from small ships. Unlike previous Kaman designs, the Seasprite reverted to the more conventional layout but retained the servo-flap controls which had characterised the rotor blades of all Kaman helicopters. Initially single-engined, twin-turbo power plants were substituted in all later versions of the Seasprite, the HH-2C being the first to be converted. An HH-2C gunship is illustrated.

112. The Seasprite can carry two homing torpedoes or other anti-submarine weapons. Installed above the torpedo are launchers for sonobuoys on this SH-2D.

113. The SH-2D is a further development of the SH-2C, with a high-powered search radar and ability to carry MAD and homing torpedoes under the Mark 1 LAMPS (Light Airborne Multi-Purpose System) programme. Behind the retractable main landing gear on this SH-2D are a homing torpedo and MAD 'bird'.

111

112

113

114. The Mark 1 LAMPS programme aimed to provide helicopters for anti-submarine warfare and anti-ship surveillance and targeting operations. The Seasprite fulfilled these requirements, together with SAR capability.

115. The power plant of the Seasprite is a twin General Electric T58-GE-8 installation, each turboshaft engine delivering 1,350 shp. A rescue hoist is mounted above the starboard door of this SH-2D on board USS *Harold E. Holt*.

Overleaf

116. An interim version of the SH-2 Seasprite, prior to the SH-2F, was this YSH-2E which retained the original landing gear. The later Seasprite SH-2F has strengthened landing gear, shortened wheelbase and -8F engines. Four passengers can be carried, in addition to the crew of three.

114

115

**Sikorsky S-61, SH-3, HSS-2, Sea King, 1959.
117.** In 1957, the US Navy had a requirement for a high performance, advanced technology helicopter to replace the S-58. Sikorsky proposed for a twin-turbine aircraft with an amphibious hull and retractable main wheels mounted on sponsons. With four hours' endurance and all-weather capability, became the S-61 submarine hunter/killer, equipped with dunking sonar and homing torpedoes. At first designated HSS-1 and later SH-3A, named Sea King, it joined the US Navy in 1961. It is powered by two 1,250 shp General Electric T58-GE-8 turboshaft engines. The fully articulated main rotor has five blades, folded hydraulically. The tail boom is foldable. A total of 265 SH-3A was built initially, nine converted to RH-3As for mine-sweeping purposes. Twelve S-61Rs became HH-3A battlefield rescue helicopters, with important modifications. In 1966, the SH-3D appeared, powered by 1,490 shp T58-GE-10 engines. Later versions include the SH-3G and H, the latter built by Agusta. The SH-3D illustrated is operated by the Peruvian Navy.

**Sikorsky S-64 Tarhe, CH-54, Skycrane, 1959.
118.** Like a gigantic insect, named after Tarhe ('Crane'), a Wyandot Indian chief of Ohio in 1795,

116

117

it was a true 'flying crane'. It was not much more than a control cabin with a rearwards-looking observation position and a six-blade main rotor, twin turboshaft engines and tail rotor. The high stalky landing gear could be raised or lowered, allowing the S-64 to crouch on the load it was to pick up. Powered by two 4,500 lb hp Pratt & Whitney JFTD12 turboshafts, the S-64 could carry 20,000 lb externally, including bulldozers, trucks and tanks. A small number used by the US First Cavalry Division in Vietnam. Invaluable, they recovered more than 380 damaged aircraft.

Gyrodyne DASH QH-50A, 1960.
119. On 12 August 1960 Gyrodyne's DSN-1 (later QH-50A) made the world's first free flight of an unmanned (drone) helicopter. It went into production as part of the US Navy's DASH (Drone Anti-Submarine Helicopter) programme. Some 750 were produced as QH-50Cs and Ds, differing chiefly in the power of their Boeing T50 turboshaft engine (270 and 300 shp respectively). Each carried two Mk 44 homing torpedoes, had a sea-level top speed of 80-103 kt and an operational radius of 30 nautical miles or more.

118

119

Boeing Vertol CH-47, HC Mk 1 Chinook, 1961.
120. The US Army's need for a heavy-lift helicopter became apparent in the course of the Korean war and, when the Vertol Aircraft Corporation was formed in 1956, their design teams began to develop two twin tandem rotor designs. The smaller type 107 at first attracted the attention of the Army but its choice fell on the larger type 114. Later named Chinook, it first

joined the US Army at the end of 1962 and operated in Vietnam as a heavy-lift helicopter.

121. Nearly a thousand Chinooks have been ordered from Boeing Vertol and the Meridionali Division of Agusta in Italy. The basic US model is the 114. The international military model, the 414, has been produced in equivalent versions. An Agusta-built CH-47C is illustrated.

122. Although the Chinook was originally classed as a heavy-lift helicopter, considerably larger aircraft have since been brought into service and the Chinook is now in the medium category. The Chinook HC Mk 1 used by the RAF is capable of carrying an armoured personnel carrier.

123. The current CH-47D is the basis of a major programme in which older models are stripped

120

121

down and rebuilt. It has a lifting capacity of 28,000 lb, more than double the capacity of the A model and more than its own empty weight. Army battlefield support is the Chinook's main function, including troop and artillery movement and battlefield resupply. The normal load is 44 troops although the only RAF Chinook to reach the Falklands in the 1982 campaign once lifted double this number. During the evacuation of Beirut, Chinooks lifted Army scout cars to ships lying offshore, as seen here.

124. A typical load for the CH-47D is a 155 mm howitzer, with 32 rounds of ammunition and an eleven-man gun crew, a combined load of about 10 tons. Using the centre of three under hooks, it can carry a 24,750 lb bulldozer. The CH-47D is powered by two 3,750 shp Avco Lycoming T55-L-712 turboshafts, capable of delivering emergency power of 4,500 shp. A programme is under way to equip Chinooks with fibre rotor blades.

122

123

124

Sikorsky S-61R, CH-3, HH-3 'Jolly Green Giant', 1963.
125. First flown in civil form in 1963, the S-61R is a version of the Sea King family with a larger fuselage, a 'kneeling' undercarriage and a rear-loading ramp. Able to carry up to 30 troops, the CH-3C and E, with two 1,300 shp T58-GE-1 turboshaft engines, was ordered by the US Air Force and re-engined with the 1,500 shp GE-5

engine. The HH-3C and E were used by the USAF for rescue work in the Vietnam war. These aircraft were given armour protection in vital parts, defensive armament and refuelling probe.

126. The US Coast Guard, with its vast coastline, also uses the similar, radar-equipped HH-3F with a radome beneath the port side windscreen. The HH-3F has the name Pelican and retains the

ability to alight on water, as shown by this Agusta-built HH-3F of the Italian air force.

Hughes (now McDonnell Douglas) 500M series, OH-6 Cayuse, 1963.
127. The OH-6 Cayuse is the military variant of the compact turbine powered Hughes 500. Originally insufficiently robust and lacking in stability and field of view for the British Army

125

which evaluated it in 1966, improvements were made and it was successfully exported for military and naval use, in the latter case carrying two Mark 44 torpedoes and MAD gear. Developments resulted in the widely used 500MD Defender series and 530MG Defender 1 and 2 series. The engine is a 317 shp Allison 250-C18A turboshaft, derated to 278 shp.

Sikorsky S-65 Sea Stallion, CH-53E 'Super Jolly', 1964.
128. Experience in the South Pacific area emphasised the need for heavy lift helicopters and, in 1962, the S-65A (then the largest helicopter designed by Sikorsky) was ordered for the US Marines. Operation of the S-64 flying crane resulted in many components being used in the S-65. A rear ramp with loading winches, enabled

the CH-53A Sea Stallion to accommodate a half-ton vehicle, a 105 mm howitzer, a Hawk or Honest John missile or slung load.

129. For transport or casevac duties, 38 troops or 24 stretchers could be carried by models of the CH-53 up to the D version, all of which were

Continued overleaf

127

128

129

129. Continued
called Sea Stallion. When unoccupied by passengers, the CH-53 had displayed astonishing agility, performing loops and rolls. Variants used by the USAF for casevac and SAR purposes were the HH-53B and C, and they became known as the 'Super Jolly Green Giant'. These variants were powered by two General Electric T64 turboshafts

of up to 3,925 shp. The CH-53E (illustrated) brought about a major improvement. It was powered by three General Electric T64-GE-416 turboshafts of 4,380 shp each, with a dramatic increase in performance. It provided a massive increase of capability for the US Marine Corps and Navy. The CH-53E can carry up to 64 troops a 32,000 lb slung load, like the 16-ton tank, illustrated. The CH-53E is named the Super

Stallion. A version of the CH-53E, the CH-53G, is used by the German Army.

Sikorsky S-65, MH-53E Sea Dragon.
130. Awesome in appearance and justifying its name is the MH-53E Sea Dragon, developed from the CH-53E. This massive helicopter is used by the US Navy as a minesweeper and tows a hydrofoil sled through the water. The example illustrated

has enlarged fuel-carrying sponsons. The canted tail rotor assists in longitudinal as well as directional trimming.

Bell 209, 309, AH-1 HueyCobra, SeaCobra, KingCobra, 1965.

131. The formidable 'gunship' version of the Huey family, the Bell HueyCobra came into being as a groundfire suppressor in support of transport helicopters. The importance of such a heavily-armed vehicle became obvious in Vietnam where the North Vietnamese troops started shooting down American troop-carrying helicopters. The two-seat Bell Model 209 attack aircraft embodied the rotor system of the UH-1 with the power plant of the UH-1C plus a new, slim fuselage. The AH-1 carries a chin turret with either a 30 mm or 20 mm three-barrelled gun or a 40 mm grenade-launcher. It is built in single and twin-engined versions, as illustrated, the upper being the twin.

132. The HueyCobra is produced in the twin-engined version as the SeaCobra for the US Marines. Developed from the AH-1J SeaCobra, the more recent AH-1T (illustrated) carries four rocket-launcher pods.

131

132

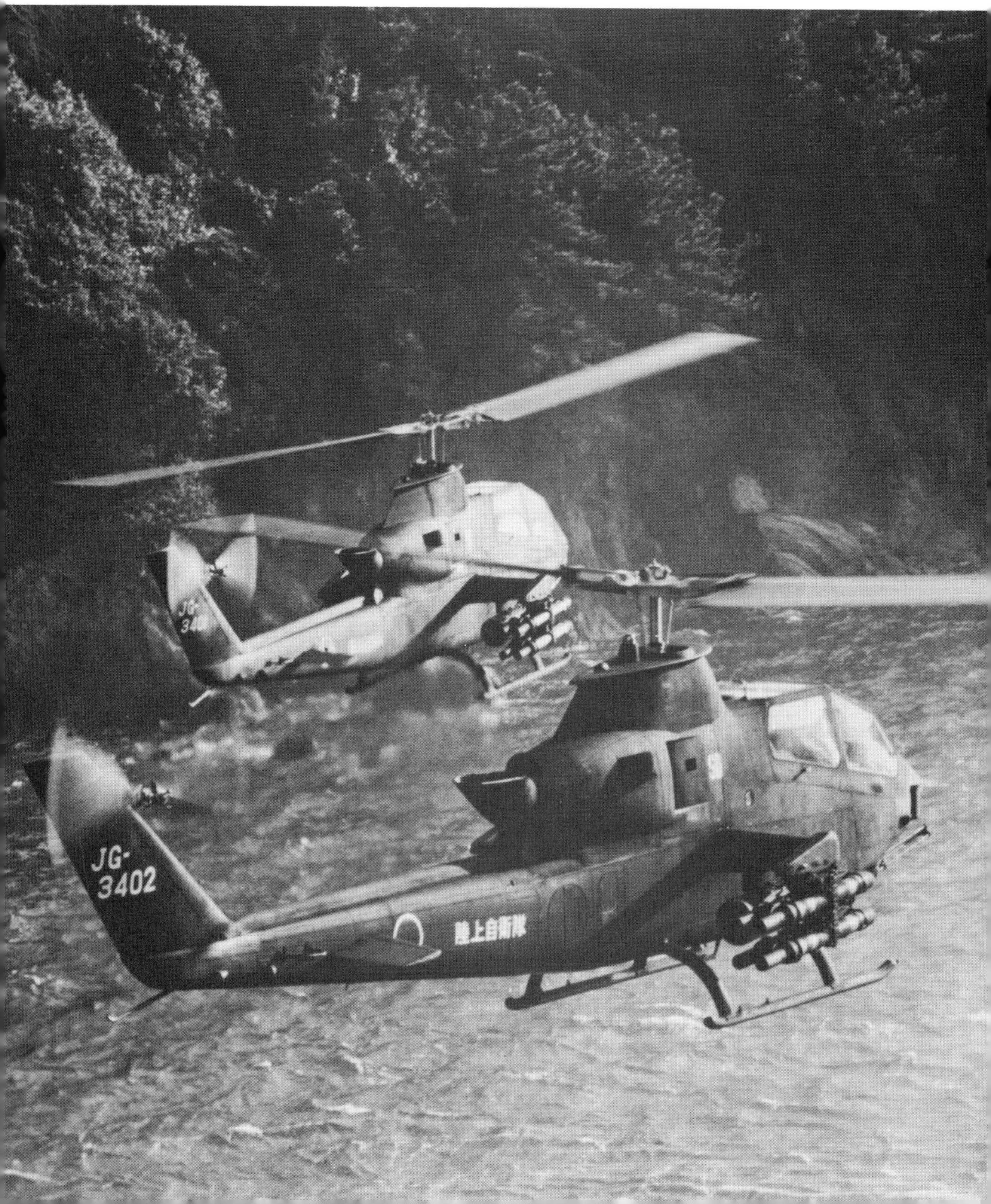
JG-
3402
陸上自衛隊

133. The HueyCobra can, in addition to its chin turret, carry eight TOW anti-tank missiles, mounted on stub wings. The slender fuselage of the HueyCobra allows the maximum speed and the heaviest possible armament compatible with crew efficiency. Its formidable armoury includes the Hellfire missile. The helicopters illustrated are AH1-S (modernised) aircraft operated by the Japanese armed forces.

134. Widely used by the US Army, the AH-1S uses the rotor system of the Model 412 and for operations in darkness or thick weather, has an FLIR (Forward Looking Infra-Red) sight which enables the gunner to see through darkness, smoke and haze. The laser range-finder is accurate to ten kilometres (six miles) and the turret position is controlled by the pilot or co-pilot/gunner through helmet sights. AIM-9 Sidewinder air-to-air missiles can also be fitted. Later versions of the AH-1S have flat plate canopies, as seen here.

135. The single-engined HueyCobra is powered by an 1,800 shp Avco Lycoming T53-L turboshaft. The twin-engined version has Pratt & Whitney Canada T400-WV-402 units totalling 2,050 shp.

136. The experimental AH-1T proposed SuperCobra prototype (illustrated) incorporated the Hughes 'Black Hole' infra-red suppression system in the exhaust. Another experimental development, the Model 249 has the standard rotor replaced by a four-blade unit, increasing agility and control power and reducing the external noise. Efforts are being made to reduce the characteristic thumping noise of the Huey's rotor.

Bell 206A, OH-58, H-57, Kiowa, JetRanger, SeaRanger, 1966.
137. The Bell 206 JetRanger was the eventual winner in 1968 of the US Army's competition for a Light Observation Helicopter. A conversion of the civil version, the military JetRanger has been built in very large numbers for the US services. An OH-58A with rotary 7.62 mm M-27 Miniguns is illustrated. The major version of the Model 206 (a

135

136

137

total of some 7,500 has been built) is the series III, or OH-58C. The armament for this version, which has seats for six passengers, is two 7.62 mm M-27 Miniguns. The power plant is one 420 shp Allison T63-A-720 turboshaft. Amongst many exported are those used by the Royal Swedish Navy. The Hughes Night Vision System (HNVS) reduces a pilot's work load on low-level missions at night, in adverse weather or in hazy and smoky conditions. An FLIR image is projected onto the pilot's helmet visor of the world outside. The pilot's head movements are relayed through a servo linkage to the FLIR turret below the helicopter, which is automatically aimed along his line of sight.

Lockheed AH-56 Cheyenne, 1967.
138. A compound helicopter embodying a forward-thrust propeller and small fixed wings in order to unload the main rotor and also to achieve high forward speeds, the Cheyenne was also notable for its rigid main and tail rotors. It was a powerful battlefield attack helicopter and the US Army at first wanted to buy 375 of them. It was, however, both complicated and expensive

and was not adopted for production or service with the US armed forces.

Sikorsky S-67 Blackhawk, 1970.
139. The S-67 was designed as an anti-tank gunship, using the dynamic components of the S-61 and a number of features of a contender for the US Army's Advanced Aerial Fire Support System (AAFSS) competition of 1965. It had low

frontal area and low drag and detachable outer stub wings with speed brakes on upper and lower surfaces. The wings had attachment points for sixteen TOW or for Swingfire anti-tank missiles. The Blackhawk — not to be confused with today's S-70 of similar name — had great agility, in addition to enormous hitting power, carrying 2.75-inch unguided rockets in eight nineteen-round pods on each wing. In addition, a

138

139

turret-mounted rotary cannon and grenade launchers could be fitted, as can be seen in the formidable armoury on this Blackhawk.

Hughes (now McDonnell Douglas) 500MD series Defender, 1974.
140. The Model 500MD is the military version of the civil D variant. This is an extremely compact helicopter and has been developed over several years into an effective and agile nap-of-the-earth attack vehicle with mast-mounted weapon sights. Renamed Defender, all military variants from the D onwards have Hughes 'Black Hole' exhaust heat suppressors, resembling rearward-facing nostrils. A Kenyan Army example is illustrated.

141. The nose-mounted stabilised optical sight is apparent on this Israeli Air Force 500MD/TOW Defender. Two TOW anti-tank missiles are mounted in pods on either side. Numerous combinations of weaponry can be carried by this compact little helicopter.

140

141

142. The Quiet Advanced Scout version of the 500MD Defender has a four-bladed tail rotor which reduces external noise by some 50 per cent. The photograph shows the Martin Marietta mast-mounted sight which contains a laser range-finder and designator and a TV lens with multiple fields of view.

143. The maritime version of the Defender, the 500MD / ASW, can mount a homing torpedo, MAD and the appropriate radar for hunting submarines.

Hughes (now McDonnell Douglas) AH-64 Apache, 1975.
144. The Apache is a second generation battlefield attack helicopter. Following the success of the HueyCobra series, Bell and Hughes responded to a US Army requirement for a substantial step forward in attack capability in all weathers by day and night. In a competition between the Bell YAH-63 and Hughes YAH-64 Apache, the Apache won. Rockets and laser-guided Hellfire missiles can be carried (sixteen, when no other rockets are carried). The 30 mm Chain-gun is chin-mounted and provided with 1,200 rounds and fires a devastating 625 rounds per minute.

145, 146. Infra-red source suppression is the purpose of the triple heat diffusers in the exhaust on either side of the Apache.

147. The advanced equipment provided in the Apache includes a Pilot's Night Vision Sensor (starboard turret) and a Target Acquisition and Designation Sight (port turret) which make possible bad weather and night operations. The latter is the gunner's principal aid, and includes direct view optics, Forward-Looking Infra-Red, TV and laser designator, range-finder and tracker. This is an expensive kit but, as enemy armour is expected to operate under the worst possible conditions to attempt to achieve surprise it becomes ever more necessary.

148. Much emphasis has been placed on an ability to survive direct hits on vital components and the Apache is capable of flight in negative 'g' conditions.

147

148

149. The Apache is powered by two 1,696 shp General Electric T700-GE-701 turboshafts.

150. A noteworthy feature of the Apache is ease of maintenance in the field.

Sikorsky S-70, H-60A Black Hawk, 1976.
151. The US Army used helicopters extensively in the course of the Vietnam war and a great fleet of Bell Hueys of various types (some 4,000) is still in use. A competition to find an eventual replacement for them was announced in 1972. Sikorsky built three prototypes to fulfil the Utility Tactical Transport Aircraft System (UTTAS) requirements. The first prototype flew in 1974.

Designated the YUH-60A and named Black Hawk, it won the competition. A production run of 1,100 H-60As and derivatives is expected to be exceeded.

149

150

151

152. In addition to a crew of three, the Black Hawk can carry at least eleven troops. As shown, a cargo hook below the cg enables the UH-60A to lift 8,000 lb. Its low profile enables it to be carried in C-130, C-141 and C-5 transports, the last being able to carry six. The movable tailplane adjusts trim in the hover.

153. The Black Hawk carries a formidable armoury of fire-suppression and anti-tank weapons, including sixteen Hellfires which can be fired in hover or even on the ground. It is in widescale use by US Army Airborne infantry units.

152

153

154. In support of anti-tank missiles, M56 mine dispensers and fire-suppression machine guns, the External Stores Support System may be attached in 40 minutes. It can carry long-range fuel tanks giving the Black Hawk a ferry range that enables it to cross the Atlantic by stages without air-to-air refuelling. The aircraft has an outstanding ability to survive in the event of battle damage.

Sikorsky S-76, H-76 Eagle, 1977.

155. Designated Armed Utility Helicopter, Eagle is a military development of the S-76 Mk II. It is a multi-mission helicopter capable of mounting eight TOW anti-tank missiles on each side or Miniguns or rockets. It can carry seven troops and is powered by two 650 shp Allison 250-C30s or two Pratt & Whitney PT6B-36s. It is proposed to incorporate a composite rotor head and all-composite blades.

154

155

Sikorsky S-70L, SH-60B Seahawk, LAMPS Mark III, 1979.
156. The US Navy's Light Airborne Multi-Purpose System (LAMPS) programme, which had started with the Kaman SH-2D Seasprite as LAMPS Mark I, was developed via the abandoned Mark II to the Mark III for which the Sikorsky SH-60 Seahawk was offered to the US Navy in 1977 in competition with Boeing Vertol. Each manufacturer submitted a development of its UTTAS project for obvious economy reasons. Sikorsky was named the winner with its S-60B, an intimate view of which appears here. The Seahawk differs from the Army Black Hawk in having a folding tail and automatic main rotor folding system. It also has a modified landing gear with shorter wheelbase and 'in hover' refuelling capability in addition to the up to date ASV and ASW equipment. Also to be seen are the two homing torpedoes and MAD 'bird' for locating and attacking submarines. The engines are 1,600 shp General Electric T700-GE-401 turboshafts.

Bell 412, OH-58D, 1979.
157. The Model 412 is the first production helicopter with a four-blade rotor to be built by Bell and is a development of the twin-turbine Model 212. The latest in the long-running 'Huey' line, it can carry fourteen troops. Its new rotor gives it greater battlefield agility and also makes it quieter than its predecessors. The power plant is two Pratt & Whitney PT6T-3B turboshaft, each

of 1800 shp. The rotor blades can be folded fore and aft. In addition to the usual assortment of battlefield attack weapons, the 412 can mount four Sea Skua or similar air-to-surface missiles. The Model 412 is also built under licence by Agusta as the Griffon (illustrated). It was flown for the first time in 1982.

Bell 406, OH-58D, AHIP, 1983.
158. In 1981, Bell won a US Army Helicopter Improvement Program (AHIP) to upgrade nearly 600 OH-58A Kiowa scout helicopters to OH-58D standard between 1985 and 1991, for close-combat reconnaissance / surveillance and intelligence-gathering. New features are a four-blade rotor and a mast sight for two lightweight air-to-air missiles.

157

Bell 406CS, OH-58D, Combat Scout, AHIP, 1983.
159. The Model 406CS (Combat Scout) is Bell's export counterpart to the OH-58D. It omits the mast-mounted sight and certain avionics but it can carry four TOW 2 anti-tank missiles or a mixture of air-to-air missiles, 2.75-inch rockets and 7.62 mm machine guns in various quick-change combinations.

Sikorsky S-70, HH-60A Night Hawk, 1984.
160. The US Air Force issued a contract to Sikorsky in 1982 for an all-weather combat rescue helicopter based on the Army's UH-60A Black Hawk. So as to replace the HH-53 Super Jolly, the proposed HH-60D had extra tanks, refuelling probe, as seen here, rescue hoist and the more powerful 1,690 shp General Electric T700-GE-401 turboshaft engines of the Seahawk. The Night

Hawk, as the US Air Force named the HH-60D, was a hybrid of the Black Hawk and Seahawk. The Air Force required specialised and expensive electronics, incorporating a Forward-Looking Infra-Red sensor, but this met Congressional opposition on the grounds of expense. As a compromise, a reduced-capability version was requested, the HH-60E, but this too was cancelled, in 1984. The proposed HH-60A, which

159

160

will be able to perform an unescorted day/night rescue mission over a radius of 285 miles at treetop level without refuelling and will be able to carry ten passengers, first flew in 1984. It is a modified UH-60A, with 1,690 shp T700-GE-401 turboshafts.

Sikorsky S-75, ACAP, 1984.
161. Sikorsky's twin-turbine S-75, first flown in July 1984, has already bettered the Advanced Composite Airframe Program (ACAP) objectives, but both contenders had an unusual problem. Although strong, composites are also brittle and could shatter in, say, a lightning strike; yet, to reinforce them with metal would seriously compromise their radar 'transparency'.

Bell D292, ACAP, 1985.
162. The U.S. Army's ACAP aims to develop more effective helicopters by using materials such as Kevlar, carbon fibre and glass fibre to reduce weight, cost and radar detectability. Bell's D292 prototype uses engines and transmission of the commercial Model 222 and is designed to survive a 42 ft/sec vertical crash.

161

162

Hughes (now McDonnell Douglas) 530MG series Defender, 1984.

163. The latest in the long and successful line of turbine-driven light helicopters in the 500 series is the 530MG Defender. A very agile example of the breed, the 530MG is a multi-role aircraft designed for battlefield operations with a mast weapons sight, enabling it to operate in nap-of-the-earth conditions. Mast sight and FLIR are customer options at present. Its weapons include TOW, 7.62 mm or 0.50-inch gun pods and seven or twelve tube launchers for 2.75-inch rockets. For naval uses, Over The Horizon (OTH) targeting capability is being developed. Seen here, a 530MG Defender launches a TOW missile using its MMS, while taking cover behind a tree. Powered by an Allison 250-C30 turbine providing 650 shp, this tadpole-like vehicle stems from the 500E, having a longer fuselage than earlier models and is the military version of the commercial 530.

6

**BLANDFORD WAR
PHOTO-FILES**

SOVIET UNION

Mil Mi-1 *Hare*, 1948.

164. Contemporary and similar to the Sikorsky S-51 and Bristol Sycamore, the Mi-1 was used in numbers by the Soviet armed forces and exported widely to east European countries and other parts of the world within the Soviet sphere of influence. It was powered by a 575hp Ivchenko AI-26V radial engine and could carry a crew of three. The largest single user, as illustrated here, was the DOSAAF para-military flying organisation, which employed the Mi-1 extensively (and still does) for civil and military helicopter crew training. Other duties included liaison and medevac.

Bratukhin Omega series, 1948.

165. Unsuccessful in a 1947 design competition for a three-seat helicopter, the Bratukhin B-10 and B-11 Omega series used twin outrigger rotors (inspired by the remarkably successful Focke-Achgelis designs) with load bearing wings indicative of the advanced thinking of Soviet and German helicopter designers. The engines were Ivchenko AI-26GR units of 575 hp mounted at the wing-tips. After vibration problems and an accident, the development programme was abandoned in 1950.

164

Mil Mi-4 *Hound*, 1952.
166. First flown in May 1952 and in Soviet service by August 1953, the Mil Mi-4 *Hound* initially had the same transmission (with different rotor blades) as the Yak-24, but underwent constant redesign until 69-foot diameter all-metal blades became standard in about 1956. Powered by an eighteen-cylinder 1,700 hp ASh-82V radial engine, it had a gross weight of 17,200 lb (payload 3,835 lb) and a top speed of 130 mph. Several thousand were built, including exports to over 30 countries, notably WARPAC nations, India, China and Cuba. Some were adapted for close support, but were not very successful in this role. It served with components of the V-VS. Its basic crew was two pilots and one or more observers gunners, Since it could be armed with a machine gun or air-to-surface rockets. A widely used general purpose helicopter, the Mi-4 could carry a crew of two and up to fourteen armed troops, a GAZ-69 jeep. a 76 mm anti-tank gun or motor-cycle combination. In naval service with the AV-MF, the *Hound-B* anti-submarine version (illustrated), with an under-nose radome and an MAD 'bird' stowed aft of the cabin, could carry sonobuoys, markers and torpedoes. It is now largely replaced by the Ka-25 and Mi-14.

165

166

167. China's People's Liberation Army received about half of the 1,000 Mi-4s built in that country as the Harbin Z-5, and still has over 300 in service. An unusual variation on some examples is a single nosewheel instead of the two separate wheels on standard Mi-4s.

Kamov Ka-15 *Hen*, 1952.
168. Used by the Soviet Navy from about 1955, the two-seat Ka-15 *Hen* could carry two depth charges for anti-submarine operations. It was the first truly operational Kamov co-axial helicopter and the ancestor of Kamov's capable ship-borne ASW helicopters of today. The engine was a 255 hp Ivchenko AI-14V radial.

Yakovlev Yak 24 *Horse*, 1952.
169. A twin-tandem rotor helicopter, the Yak-24 was the first serious attempt by the Yakovlev Design Bureau to produce a troop and cargo-carrying helicopter, but was an early victim of serious ground resonance problems. Like the contemporary British Belvedere, its V tail later gave way to a straight tailplane with endplates. The Yak-24U production version, which could

167

carry 40 armed soldiers, was powered by two 1,700 hp ASh-82V radial engines. It was used by the Soviet Air Force in small numbers but was not particularly successful. Production in all was about 100, including civil examples.

Mil Mi-6 *Hook*, 1957.
170. When it first appeared in 1957 the Mi-6 was the world's largest helicopter. It is capable of carrying 70 soldiers or 41 stretchers plus two medical attendants. The five-blade rotor is turned by two 5,500 shp Soloviev D25V turboshaft engines. The Mi-6 first came into prominence in the Arab-Israeli war of June 1967 when several were destroyed on the ground. The

Mi-6 has a very large capacity cabin, 12 metres (39.4 feet) long, and can carry trucks or cargo instead of troops. Nearly 1,000 are believed to have been built, of which about 400 are still in SovAF service and others with the air forces of Algeria, Egypt, Iran, Peru and Vietnam.

169

170

Mil Mi-8 *Hip*, c.1960.

171. Mil's Mi-8, in service from the early 1960s, has proved an immensely successful second-generation successor to the Mi-4. Known to NATO as *Hip* (this is a *Hip-C* basic assault transport), it is powered by two 1,500 shp TV2-117A turbine engines instead of the single 1,700 hp piston radial of the Mi-4. Empty weight is less than 25 per cent up on the Mi-4, but payload is doubled from fourteen to 28 troops or 8,820 lb of internal cargo. Its cabin gives 17 ft 6 ins of clear space, making it a useful battlefield support helicopter. Armament can be rocket or gun pods. Mi-8s serve with 40 or more air forces as well as with Soviet forces, and well over 10,000 (military and civil) have been built during the past quarter-century.

172. Among over 40 services operating Mil Mi-8s is the little known air force of Guinea-Bissau. The Doppler radar box under the tailboom is a standard feature of all *Hip* variants except the *Hip-K* ECM (communications jamming) version. This is a *Hip-C*.

171

172

Mil Mi-8 *Hip-F*, 1960.
173. *Hip-E* and *Hip-F* versions of the Mi-8 (this is an *F*) are the most heavily armed helicopters in the world, carrying no fewer than 192 rockets in six launchers, with four *Swatter* anti-tank missiles (E) or six *Saggers* above them, plus nose gun. In 1985, some 1,600 Mi-8s were in service with Soviet armies in the field. The uprated Mi-17 *Hip-H*, which has two 1,900 shp Isotov TV3-117MT

turboshaft engines in shorter nacelles, and a port side tail rotor like that of the Mi-14, is now beginning to replace the Mi-8, offering a considerable improvement in performance. It is basically a freight carrier, with the same payloads of 8,820 lb (internal) or 6,615 lb (external). Full three-axis stability, both in flight and during the hover, make either type a valuable battlefield workhorse.

Kamov Ka-25 *Hormone*, C. 1960.
174. Over 450 twin-turbine Kamov Ka-25s (NATO *Hormone*) were produced during 1966-75, replacing modified Mi-4s for ship and shore-based ASW duties *(Hormone-A)*, missile targeting/guidance *(Hormone-B)* and search/rescue/utility roles *(Hormone-C* illustrated on board *Minsk)*. Small numbers were exported.

173

174

175. Anti-submarine *Hormone-As* are based aboard the carrier/cruisers *Kiev, Kharkov, Minsk, Novorissiysk* and, in a mix with *Hormone-Bs,* in the *Leningrad* and *Moskva,* the complement being eighteen to nineteen in each case. The *A* version (illustrated) has an under-nose radome, towed MAD sonobuoys and fair weather dipping sonar. *Hormone-B* is distinguished by a bigger and rounder radome, a 'dust-bin' radome under the rear fuselage and a data link to provide mid-course guidance for long-range cruise missiles such as the SS-N-3 *Shaddock,* SS-N-12 *Sandbox* and SS-N-19. Some *Hormones* carry two homing torpedoes or small 'fire and forget' air-to-surface weapons. During NATO's eight nation OCEAN SAFARI 1975 this Kamov Ka-25 from the Soviet cruiser *Admiral Isachenkov* overflew the Royal Navy's *Ark Royal,* with a Buccaneer and a Phantom.

Mil Mi-2 *Hoplite,* **1963.**
176. More than 4,700 Mi-2s, a turbine engined development of the Mi-1, have been built in Poland since 1964 for civil and military use. It is used by the armed forces of the Soviet Union, Cuba, Czechoslovakia, Poland and Romania in anti-tank, light transport and ambulance roles.

175

176

Mil Mi-12 *Homer,* 1968.
177. The huge Mi-12 was designed to support in the field the equally impressive Antonov An-22 transport. Capable of carrying a load of over 40 tonnes, the Mi-12 used two of the five-blade rotor units of the Mi-6 and was powered by four 6,500 shp Soloviev D-25VF turboshafts mounted in pairs at the ends of inversely tapered wings which unloaded the outward-turning main rotors in forward flight. Although only a prototype, with a gross weight of 231,485 lb it remains the heaviest helicopter ever flown.

Mil Mi-14 *Haze, c* 1974.
178. Developed to replace the Mi-4 in Soviet Navy service, the Mi-14 *Haze* is basically a maritime version of the Mi-8. It has a boat-shaped hull, more powerful Isotov TV3-117 turboshafts of about 1,900 shp in shorter nacelles, a port side tail rotor, fully retractable landing gear and a water rudder. The Soviet Navy has about 100 anti-submarine *Haze-A*s and ten *Haze-B*s for mine countermeasures, the latter having fuselage side-strakes and no external MAD 'bird'. *Haze-A* carries torpedoes and depth charges in the bomb bay. Mi-14s have also been supplied to Bulgaria, Cuba, East Germany, Libya and Poland.

177

178

Mil Mi-24 *Hind*, c 1972.

179. The Soviet Union's first battlefield support helicopter, the *Hind-A* entered service in East Germany in 1973-74. With the same basic power plant, rotors and transmission as the Mi-8, a four-man flight crew, it can bring eight fully-armed troops into a battle area. *Hind-A* is armed with a 12.7 mm nose gun, four *Swatter* anti-tank missiles and four underwing bombs, etc.

180. *Hind-D* carries a four-barrel 12.7 mm Gatling gun in the undernose turret, four *Swatter* anti-tank missiles on wingtip launchers and four underwing pylons for up to 1,500 kg of bombs. The pylons can also carry 128 57mm rockets, chemical weapons, etc. The weapon operator occupies the front cockpit. The gun is fully flexible. Pod fairings to each side of it house target acquisition and tracking sensors.

181. *Hind-E* a recently identified Mi-24 variant, has a port-side tail rotor, a twin-barrel cannon (probably of higher calibre than the *Hind-D's* four-barrel 12.7 mm) in a semi-cylindrical starboard fairing instead of a nose turret. It can carry four wingtip *Spiral* tube-launched, laser-homing anti-tank missiles instead of the less effective *Swatters*. It entered service with the Soviet armed forces in about 1980.

179

180

181

Mil Mi-26 *Halo, c* 1979.

182, 183. A huge transport helicopter, supported by an eight-blade rotor, the Mi-26 *Halo* made an impressive first appearance in the West at the 1981 Paris Air Show; it entered military service a year later. This 20-tonne load carrier powered by two Lotarev turboshaft engines, each delivering 11,400 shp, takes off at a weight of 123,450 lb. It is the heaviest operational helicopter ever flown, outweighed only by the prototype Mi-12, some of whose payload-to-height records it has already beaten, and can carry about 90 armed troops or two infantry combat vehicles in a cargo hold comparable in capacity to a Lockheed C-130's. Seen in the West only in *Aeroflot* livery, the Mi-26 is the first helicopter to fly successfully with an eight-blade main rotor.

184. The most formidable battlefield helicopter yet to see action against ground troops, the *Hind-D* is capable of clearing a path for tanks and troops, knocking out enemy tanks and anti-tank defences by acting as a high-speed 'tank' itself. *Hind-D*s have been employed extensively in Afghanistan by the Soviet and Afghan armies in 'COIN' operations. In 1984, they were supplied to strengthen the Sandinista strike capability.

182

183

184

Kamov Ka-27 *Helix*, 1981.
185. First revealed in 1981 in its sixteen passenger civil Ka-32 form, the twin turboshaft *Helix* was clearly destined for naval use and the existence of the Ka-27 ASW version was confirmed in 1982. Missile support and SAR/planeguard versions have been identified since, confirming *Helix* as a much improved successor to the Ka-25 *Hormone*, probably usable also for 'Vertrep' (vertical replenishment) and infantry assault. So far seen on the carrier/cruiser *Novorissiysk* and the guided missile destroyer *Udaloy*, the Ka-27 was designed to fit the same deck lifts as *Hormone* and may utilise landing gear and other components from its predecessor. The Indian Navy, already a *Hormone* operator, began to receive eighteen *Helix* in 1985.

Mil Mi-28 *Havoc*.
186. Expected to become operational in 1987-88, the Mi-28 *Havoc* two-seat battlefield helicopter is armed with a heavy-calibre nose gun and wing-mounted air-to-air or air-to-ground missiles or rockets. With armour protection, nose radar and infra-red suppressors/decoys, it should be even more effective than the Mi-24.

185

186

THE FUTURE

Eurocopter HAP, France and Germany.
187. The Franco-German Eurocopter partnership (Aérospatiale and MBB) is developing a family of three anti-tank helicopters for service in the 1990s. The French Army's HAP (illustrated), to fly in 1988, will have a 30 mm nose gun, plus two Mistral AAMs and a rocket pod under each stub-wing.

Eurocopter PAH-2, France and Germany.
188. HAP will be followed in 1993 by the German Army PAH-2 (illustrated). This will carry up to eight HOT 2 anti-tank and four Stinger 2 air defence missiles underwing, with nose-mounted sight, but has no under-nose turret. Germany will have 212 PAH-2s; France's 75 HAPs will be followed in the mid-1990s by 140 HAC-3Gs armed with eight Euromissile ATGW-3 missiles. All will

have a common basic airframe, powered by two 1,225 shp MTM 385-R turbine engines, with a two-man crew (pilot and co-pilot/gunner), 42 ft 8 in diameter main rotor and a gross weight of about 11,000 lb.

187

188

189

Sikorsky LHX Shadow, USA.
189, 190. The LHX specification calls for an 8,500
lb gross weight helicopter with a 38 ft main
rotor, twin 1,200 shp T800 turboshaft engines
with 185 US gallons of fuel and a top speed of 170
knots at maximum continuous power. It also
stipulates single-pilot operation, which explains
the rather grotesque appearance of this Sikorsky
testbed.

191. SHADOW, an acronym for Sikorsky Helicopter Advanced Demonstrator of Operator Workload, is actually a standard S-76 with an extra one-man cockpit grafted on to the nose. Cockpit equipment includes a fly-by-wire side-arm control stick, head-up display with coupled helmet display, touch sensitive CRTs, FLIR and remote map reader.

Westland/Agusta EH 101, UK/Italy.
192. The EH 101 is being developed by Westland and Agusta as a Sea King replacement for the Royal and Italian Navies, and is due to enter service in the early 1990s. Slightly smaller than the Sea King (to fit existing hangars and deck lifts), it will carry a 13,400lb payload, for a maximum take-off weight of 28,650 lb, on the power of three 1,730 shp General Electric T700 turbine engines, with a crew of one or two pilots plus an observer and acoustic systems operator. Equipment will include a 360 degree search radar, dipping sonar, sonobuoys and four Sting Ray homing torpedoes.

McDonnell Douglas LHX, USA
193. McDonnell Douglas (originally Hughes) Helicopters' entry for the LHX competition, expected to feature the company's NOTAR (no tail rotor) system of torque control, has the most futuristic appearance of any of the probable candidate designs. LHX is intended to replace four existing US Army helicopters: the UH-1, AH-1, OH-6 and OH-58.

192

193

Bell LHX, USA.
194. LHX (Light Helicopter Experimental) is the
US Army's biggest-ever aircraft programme,
requiring around 5,000 LHXs for scout/attack and
utility duties. Bell originally submitted a tilt-rotor
design, but switched to a more conventional
'penny-farthing' helicopter layout when tilt-
rotors were ruled out by the Army.

Boeing Vertol XCH-62, USA.
195. In the mid-1970s, the US Army put out proposals for a new Heavy Lift Helicopter (HLH). Boeing submitted a development of the Chinook as a 'flying crane'. It would have been capable of carrying major engineering structures, notably bridging pontoons. The project was shelved in October 1974 before it could fly, but was resuscitated in 1983 as a twin-rotor aircraft to be capable of carrying at least 20 tons over a distance of 25 miles. Boeing Vertol's three-engined, 90-foot long XCH-62 is now to fly in 1988 as a heavy lift research prototype capable of lifting a payload of half its own 140,000 lb gross weight. The diameter of each rotor is 92ft.

Bell/Boeing V-22 Osprey, USA.
196. The Bell/Boeing V-22 Osprey is planned as a joint services vertical lift aircraft for the US Navy, Marine Corps, Air Force and Army, utilising the tilt-rotor system developed in the experimental Bell XV-15. Powered by two 5,000 shp class turbine engines, it is due to fly in 1988. Requirements include 552 MV-22As as USMC assault transports and 231 for medevac/cargo

lift duties with the US Army; 80 CV-22As for USAF long-range special operations; and 50 HV-22As as combat/SAR helicopters for the US Navy. Its payload includes 24 troops or 2,880 lb of cargo.

Kamov Ka-? *Hokum* **USSR.**
197. Little is yet known about the new Kamov *Hokum* air-to-air combat helicopter. It is in the 5,500 kg gross weight class with a top speed of

350km/hr and an operational radius of 250 km, carrying a two-man crew and gun/rocket armament. Possibly less agile than the Apache, it is expected to give WARPAC nations a significant rotary-wing air superiority capability, with no current Western counterpart. The illustration is based on drawings appearing in The US Department of Defense 1985 *Soviet Military Power* booklet and later information.　M G BURNS

BIBLIOGRAPHY

Apostolo, Giorgio *World Encyclopedia of Civil and Military Helicopters*. Collins.
Gablehouse, Charles *Helicopters and Autogiros*. Muller.
Gunston, W. *Helicopters of the World*. Temple Press/Aerospace.

King, H.F., Ed Taylor, J.W.R. *Jane's 100 Significant Aircraft 1909-1969*. Jane's, London.
Munson, K. *Helicopters since 1907*. Blandford Press, Poole.
Swanborough, F.G. *US Military Aircraft since 1909*. Putnam.

Swanborough, Gordon, and Bowers, Peter M. *US Navy Aircraft since 1911*. Putnam.
Taylor, J.W.R., Munson, K. *History of Aviation*. New English Library, London.
Wragg, David *Helicopters at War*. Hale.

ACKNOWLEDGEMENTS

Help is gratefully acknowledged by the authors for the expert assistance of Ann C. Tilbury in gathering and collating the pictures, and of the Directors and staff of the following museums, for generous assistance given in researching archive materials and photographic records: The Fleet Air Arm Museum, Yeovilton; The Royal Air Force Museum, Hendon; The Army Air Corps Museum of Army Flying, Middle Wallop; Reg Mack, RAF Museum; Alan Williams, Michael J. Willis, Imperial War Museum; Major John Cross, Museum of Army Flying, as well as many others who helped.

INDEX